Made Wijaya's
TROPICAL GARDEN DESIGN

Made Wijaya's
TROPICAL GARDEN DESIGN

PERIPLUS

For my mother, Mavis White,
whose green thumb and sharp tongue
I inherited.

SPECIAL CONSULTING EDITORS: Maggie Dallmeyer, Carole Muller
PICTURE EDITOR AND CO-DIRECTOR: Marie-Claude Millet
ILLUSTRATIONS AND CO-DIRECTOR: Chang Huai-Yan
MANAGING EDITOR: Tim Jaycock
DESIGNER: Nelani Jinadasa
PRODUCTION MANAGER: Edmund Lam

PHOTOGRAPHERS:
Isabella Ginanneschi, Reto Guntli, Jerry Harpur,
Rio Helmi, Pierre Poretti, Dominic Sansoni,
Tara Sosrowardoyo, Tim Street-Porter,
Luca Invernizzi Tettoni, Laura van Wieringen,
Made Wijaya, John Witzig

Designed and produced by
Editions Didier Millet
64, Peck Seah Street, Heritage Court,
Singapore 079325

Printed in Singapore

Page 2: *Statue by Wayan Cemul in a nest of Russelia bushes at the
Four Seasons Resort, Jimbaran, Bali.*

ACKNOWLEDGEMENTS

First I must thank all the Balinese gardeners — particularly Ketut Marsa, Wayan Legawa, Dewa Putu Sedana and Dewa Made Mudita — who have taught me to be a feudal overlord — and my loyal assistants — Gusti Ngurah Sarjana, Putu Suasta, Nyoman Miyoga, Fairus Bin Salleh in Singapore and Agung Handoko in Jakarta — who have put up with the esults. Without their hard work, patience and dedication, and that of all our commando squads and our carvers (Dewa Nyoman Muka and Dewa Putu Oka in particular), many of the gardens in this book would not have been possible.

The support of two ladies of great style and enthusiasm must be mentioned up front too: Maggie Dallmeyer who believed enough in my work, and my writing, to help launch this project and see it through the difficult straits of infancy, and into adolescence; and Carole Muller, who has helped polish the text and acted as garden historian-godmother. Friend, writer and photographer Tim Street-Porter and his wife, designer Annie Kelly, have been incredibly supportive throughout my 20 years of doing gardens on Bali (and Tim was most generous with permission to use his gorgeous pictures). They, together with Putu Suarsa and Stephen Little, have been guiding lights. Christopher and Katherine Carlisle, and Ruth and Kerry Hill, were also enormously supportive during the early stages of my gardening career, and I can never thank them enough. Chris and Kerry both kindly also loaned images of their design work for this book. Luca Tettoni has allowed this book's co-director, Huai-Yan, almost unfettered access to Vivian's sliding drawers in his office; and I am eternally indebted to two brilliant Indonesian photographers, Rio Helmi and Tara Sosrowardoyo, whose drawers may not slide so easily but whose souls soar when their lenses roar. English photographer Jerry Harpur, and Pierre Poretti and Reto Guntli of Switzerland and Luc Boucharge of Paris were also very generous in the loaning of beautiful images, as was Dutch publisher Peter de Bont, the Singapore Botanic Gardens and Sri Lankan Dominic Sansoni. To the painters who have captured my work with eye-opening accuracy — Sakiko Ibuchi of Japan; Cressida Campbell, Stephen Little and Peter Wright of Australia; and Nigel Waymouth of the U.K., I take off my hat. I thank Australian painting legend Margaret Olley for her gracious permission to reproduce a painting of hers and Brian Moore of the Australia Galleries in Sydney who, with the trustees of the Arnott Estate, helped in obtaining permission to reproduce a painting by Donald Friend of an early Batu Jimbar garden. My gratitude also to James Fairfax for providing some early (1972) photographs of Donald Friend's Sanur garden. Hawaiian master landscaper Ray Cain and Waimea landscaper Robert Frost were very generous with information on the Hawaiian section also. For William Warren's words of wisdom and most gracious and sportsman-like horticultural advice I am profoundly grateful. The support and grace of Kim Inglis must be mentioned here, too. Publisher Hans Höfer was an enthusiastic adviser from the start of this project, as was James Dallmeyer and Terry Fripp, my Singapore friends, and Lady Amabel Lindsay and Caroline Younger in London. Special thanks to Francois Richli, Esq. of the Amanjiwa and Mercedes Zobel-Pessina for permission to produce photographs of their sumptuous properties; to Yu-Chee Chong in London for loaning a 19th-century print; and to the architect greats Geoffrey Bawa and Peter Muller who have been quietly supportive over the years (many of their master works are cribbed on the pages of this book).

Truly profound thanks to Chang Huai-Yan my student who became this book's illustrator, and co-director, with the lovely Marie-Claude Millet, and the enormously patient and talented Nelani Jinadasa.

To Tim Jaycock and all the wonderful team at Editions Didier Millet, particularly Didier, I offer my heartfelt thanks for helping see this project through.

To my Wijaya Words staff in Bali — the tireless Sri Sudewi, Agus Perry, Putu Semiada and Kadek Wirawan — I profess undying gratitude.

C O N T E N T S

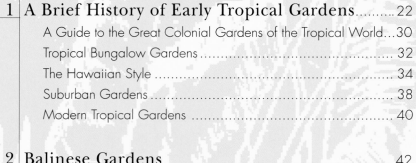

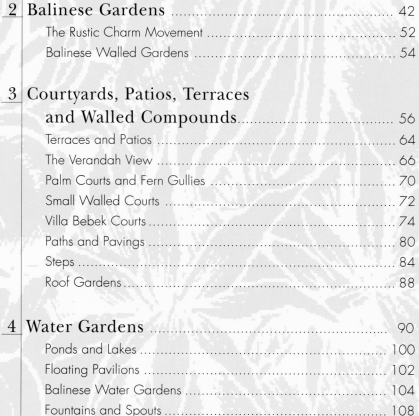

INTRODUCTION

A Dutch friend of mine once remarked that she loved the Tropics because "all the indoor plants were on the outside". I stumbled upon a career as a tropical garden designer with the same sort of wide-eyed amazement: the exotic lushness of tropical gardens, the palms, ferns and wild colours were a source of wonder for someone used to the muted hues and sparseness of Australia.

Over 25 years of making gardens in various tropical locales, this wonder has grown into a deep respect. It is the sort of respect that an animal trainer has for a wild beast. For tropical gardens, be they in the Philippines, the Caribbean, Florida or Northern Queensland, all have one thing in common: the tendency to get out of control. The phrase "ordered jungle" was used some time ago to describe my work at the Bali Hyatt hotel in Sanur. Keeping a tropical garden on that edge of fecundity (before it turns to an unsightly mess) is hard work. Taking on the care of a tropical garden is taking on maintenance.

A garden is much more than the sum of its plants. A well-composed garden, tropical or otherwise, first complements the architecture or landscape to which it is attached, then creates a story — what the Japanese call a *tagachi* or "point of view" — that involves all the elements, the paths, ponds, outdoor furniture, accents and lighting.

It is my hope, in this book, to impart some of my experience gained from creating over 400 gardens in the tropical world, and some of the artistic knowledge I've picked up admiring other people's work.

Travel has been my best teacher and I include here a wide range of references to inspire both the beginner and professional — from the Hawaiian style, through the various "ornamental Oriental" looks, to the Modern Movement popular in Singapore and Rio de Janeiro.

Balinese culture with its love of observing, absorbing, adapting and adopting has been a great teacher too. Every Balinese temple is an extraordinary garden — a sublimely beautiful mix of ornamental trees and shrubs, and sculpture-like buildings. Ponds, carved walls and grassy expanses are occasional features: but it is really just the height of the temple architecture artistry and the garden inventiveness that reward the senses. The Balinese culture puts the holy alliance of religion, nature and art above all else, so it is not surprising that one finds so much inspiration in the thousands of temples of Bali, and to an extent, the remains of the Hindu *candi* in Java.

However, in this admiration for the artworks and the architecture, the garden designer must keep an eye on the balance with "the growies", as plants are affectionately called by Australian architects. A garden designer must love nature and learn how to create nature. The "edge of

---

OPPOSITE: Amanbrioche Cottage at Taman Bebek, a small hotel I designed in Bali. BELOW, LEFT AND RIGHT: The beautiful 16th-century Candi Sukuh, near Solo, the last temple of Java's Hindu era; a megalithic village square on Sumba, East Indonesia.

PAGE 5: The view from the author's desk, at the Villa Bebek, Sanur, Bali. PAGES 8–9: A verandah and garden in the Villa Bebek. PAGES 10–11: The parklands of the Bali Hyatt hotel in Sanur.

fecundity" and the "freshness" of originality go hand in hand in any good tropical garden. Observing the way plants grow in different soil conditions and in different light is half of the artistry of good garden design in any climate. In the Tropics, where there are not four distinct seasons, but most often a wet (monsoon) and a dry (hot) season, the sun often races from 22° north in the sky to 22° south every six months. Any planting under a north- or south-facing eave, for example, must be tolerant of both shade- and full sun. A very tall order!

Water plants have fallow periods which are hard to dictate, as do Plumerias and night blooming cestrum, for example. Whereas there are shrubs and vines, such as Gardenias, Allamanda and the Stephanotis, which flower best in the wet season. Bougainvillea, Hibiscus and Thunbergia thrive in a dry heat. Finally, everything seems to come on again for good

luck when the sun finally appears after a long monsoon. Good soil conditions too are important, especially for palms and sensitive ground covers, and for the control of tropical blights and fungi.

This book will attempt to lead you down the garden path, as it were, past the shady terraces, mossy walls and statues, leafy water gardens, Bougainvillea-strewn trellises, glistering pools and well-swept courtyards that make up the tropical garden world. While you walk I hope you will learn and soon know the joy of creating a garden in the Tropics.

As "theatrical nature" is my middle name, I will further attempt to show ways of giving a terrace or a courtyard a "romantic" look by introducing a decorative or ornamental theme — Balinese, Japanese or Moorish. However, I will emphasize that a garden should be judged by its completeness, its harmony with nature, its surroundings (the balance of the man-made and the natural), as much as its theatrical appeal. "Ordered jungle" and "spooky" are both terms that have been used to describe my work: one man's pudding is another's poison, I guess.

People born in tropical climes tend to be less enamoured of leafy profusion, preferring more light and air to move through the garden. Through history, the peoples of the Tropics have had to fight back the jungle: I remember on my first trip to Thailand, in 1980, being shocked at the proliferation of dwarf plants, herbaceous borders and topiary Bambis. Rolf Von Beuren, who with his wife Helen created one of the great tropical oases (now in a concrete canyon in downtown Bangkok), explained to me that the Thais had spent hundreds of years fighting back nature and therefore now tended towards "over-control" in garden design. Halting the

BELOW: An austerely beautiful temple backed by a forest of tropical bamboo high in the mountains of Bali. Ancient tropical gardens such as this are, for the most part, bereft of ornamental plantings.

ABOVE RIGHT: A wildly ornamental 19th-century temple garden in the *Pura Beji*, at Sangsit, on the North Coast of Bali. Chinese and colonial influences can be discerned in both the architecture and the landscape design.

advance of the herbaceous borders and "twee" planter boxes — the colonial retirement villages' gift to the tropical world — has become a bit of an obsession for me in my crusade against the pervading gentrified landscape aesthetic. I long for the acceptance of artful naturalism by the town planners of tropical Asia. Singapore, remarkably, is the only Southeast Asian country to date to adopt the natural look for its streetscapes.

My "tropical Cotswolds" style grew out of this obsession, later to be joined by various other collections that were as much a result of my travels in Southeast Asia, admiring traditional architecture, as of sitting at the feet of garden masters. The examples which illuminate various ideas in this book draw liberally from this portfolio — including the "ruinscape period", the "bleu majorelle" Moroccan period, and the "courtyard cosy" look.

Photographing traditional villages in tropical climes, from Yunnan in South China, to Irian Jaya in far eastern Indonesia and New Guinea, I have noticed that ancient gardens, where they exist, are often quite sparse. The architecture is the garden, with vast communal courts forming village-wide living rooms. Often a platform of rocks (Neolithic garden furniture) is set out in the shade under a giant canopy tree. The ancient village squares on the islands of Nias and Sumba in Indonesia are good examples of this type of landscaping (see page 13).

Tropical countries which have experienced classic civilizations — notably Kerala and Orissa in East India, Sri Lanka, Cambodia, Thailand and Indonesia — have developed cultured landscape concepts, not dissimilar to the ancient civilizations of Egypt and Mesopotamia. Water tanks, moats, reflecting pools, and pleasure gardens, are typically found in the palace gardens of these countries. Rulers' garden designers often showcased the latest trends from overseas, or copied from the neighbouring ruler's palace.

A botanical print from one of the earliest records of the tropical world. Clearly marked in Latin are the *musa* (banana) and the *ananas* (pineapple).

Many fabulous gardens survive from the 12th to 18th centuries — a golden era for landscape design. Of these gardens, my particular favourites are: the kings' bathing pavilion at Kandy in Sri Lanka, which sits on a man-made lake adjacent to the Temple of the Tooth; the vast Angkor Wat complex in Cambodia; the water follies and pleasure gardens of the kings of East Bali and Western Lombok in Indonesia; the "floating city" of Sukhothai in northern Thailand; the imperial palace in Hue, Central Vietnam and the incredible Taman Sari royal baths in the Kraton (Palace) of Sultan Hamengkubuwono in Yogyakarta, Central Java, Indonesia and the Victorian Vimarn Mek garden in Bangkok. All of these ancient tropical gardens can be considered marvels of the Indo-Chinese landscape world.

The colonial era brought a glamorous gentility to the tropical garden. During this time, neat lawns, quaint *parterres* and verandahs lined with potted plants replaced the utilitarian swept-dirt courts and living kitchen gardens. It also brought botanists from Leiden in The Netherlands (the world's first *Hortus Botanicus*) and the Royal Botanic Gardens at Kew in London, England, who established tropical botanical gardens first by Banks and Bligh in St. Vincent, the West Indies, then Peradeniya outside Kandy in Sri Lanka, at Bogor in West Java and eventually Singapore, Brisbane, Kenya and Louisiana. During the 17th and 18th centuries, the era of colonial expansion and exploitation, the Dutch *perkeneers*, the "park owners", in Java and the Spanish and English plantation owners in the Philippines and Malaysia respectively brought the art of hacienda parklands and cottage

gardening to the Tropics. Sadly, today, only in the oldest estates in the Philippines, Happy Valley in Kenya, the sugar fields of Martinique, Barbados and Jamaica and in the softly rolling hills behind Cairns, Queensland, Australia, does one still find tropical gardens in the old colonial tradition.

Today, tropical landscaping in the grand tradition of the 18th-century English masters is rare — confined, it seems, to a handful of wealthy bachelors, spread across the equator. John Allerton's remarkable garden in Kauai, Hawaii (now the Pacific Tropical Garden), and James Deering's Viscaya (designed by Columbian–born Diego Suarez) in Miami are two 20th-century masterworks of tropical landscape design. Irish Banochie's Andromeda garden in Barbados and Geoffrey Bawa's garden at Lunuganga in Sri Lanka are other splendid examples.

The most astounding of all the great American private horticultural dream gardens is the Fairchild Tropical Garden in Miami. Funded by a local philanthropist Colonel Montgomery, naturalist Captain Fairchild made many plant-collecting expeditions through the South China, Java and Banda Seas in his Chinese junk to stock this "Kew of the tropical world".

The recent age of tourism, most notably in the islands of Hawaii and Bali, has given us the sort of tropical parklands and romantic follies previously found only in the (few) tropical botanical gardens and homes of the nobility where they existed in the tropical world.

The romantic notion of the tropical lifestyle still survives, however, where in many places the old colonial bungalows and gardens have not. The impressionist painters Rousseau and Gauguin's first images fuelled the imaginations of a century of world travellers who went in search of giant leaves tended by dewy natives, as pictured. The steamy nights under the sweep of the ceiling fan, the nocturnal cicada cacophony, the coconut-palm-fringed shores and the search for the bathing spring in the forest of ferns are all part of the mystique of the tropical world.

Today's raja's follies are the six-star hotels, with their incredible grounds and trad-mod architecture. Hotels such as the Amandari and Bali Hyatt in Bali, the Shangri-La Hotel in Singapore and the Four Seasons Resort in Maui, are the New-Age temples of the tropical world. People regularly drop out to make dream homes and gardens on tropical islands, and natives of the Tropics regularly drop back in from overly urban life styles. As the legendary Basil Charles, Mustique's most famous lapsed gardener once remarked, "I don't want to go back to nature, I came from nature!"

OPPOSITE: Belgian painter Jean Le Mayeur de Merprès gave the romantic tropical garden movement impetus with his heavenly Balinese garden, on the beach, near Sanur harbour on Bali's Southeast Coast (Courtesy of Christie's Singapore). His garden was a joyous artistic oasis, brimming with ornamentation.
BELOW: Pierre Poretti's image of the Hotel Saba Bay, with gardens and architecture designed by our office, in 1985. The formal gardens were inspired by the Moghul gardens of India and the water gardens of Javanese and Balinese palaces. RIGHT: The striking Amanjiwa hotel, "the tropical world's answer to the Taj Mahal" screamed one excited pundit; a postcard from the magnificent Fairchild Tropical Garden in Miami, Florida, USA.

DEVELOPING A TROPICAL GARDEN STYLE

I arrived in Bali in 1974 as a dropout from Architectural School at Sydney University. I fell in love with an island, a culture and a family and have lived and worked on the fabled isle ever since.

In 1979, after five years of living in Bali, I was asked by Warwick Purser to design a garden for House "C" (architect Geoffrey Bawa), on the exclusive Batu Jimbar estate in Sanur. I had designed a tropical orientalist garden for myself in a burned out house in Sydney (see page 61) in 1975, during a year back at university, but had never worked professionally. To start, I asked my great chum at that time, Ketut Marsa, a rice farmer from Sidarkarya village near Sanur, to set up a two-man garden company. With the passion of converts we attacked Geoffrey Bawa's sensual courtyard

The Chinese water garden at the Bali Hyatt hotel in Sanur was much photographed during the 1980s. This image, featuring the first-ever Bali lamp, adorned the walls of the arrival hall at Bali's Denpasar airport for some years.

architecture of the Purser House. Before too long, two years in fact, we had revamped nearly all of the 10 Batu Jimbar estate gardens plus The Oberoi hotel (architect Peter Muller) as our playgrounds and it was here that Ketut and I experimented with various looks and with the ornamental use of local plants. We had tiny budgets but big hearts. We experimented with balance, composition and the "architecture" or "sculpture" of landscaping. They were happy years spent with happy people. From Ketut I learnt how to lean a frangipani (Plumeria) and from Donald Friend, the Australian artist whose own house was a shrine for lovers of romantic garden settings, I learnt how to trim them into tight, taut shapes. "The torso of the frangipani," he would say, "is the tropical world's oak." Training Bougainvillea and *Hibiscus schitzopetalus* up Plumeria trunks became my trademark at this time.

From the Balinese I learnt to be both feudal (it helps when doing big gardens) and animistic (the belief in the spirits of place). By incorporating the Balinese "take no hostages" approach to task-mastering — thus the aptly-named "commando squad" units of Balinese master gardeners — I developed a reputation as a garden artist who was part designer and part contractor. The notion of tropical gardens that were both artfully and quietly cultural took root. From Peter Muller's masterwork, the Bali Oberoi (then the Kayu Ayu), I learned about the landscaper's friend, soapstone (in Bali called *paras batu*), the pitted volcanic tuft found throughout Indonesia and the Philippines. It is economical, easy to work and unjarring to the eye in the landscape. I used this stone, routinely, on my stairs, pond edges and garden walls. From the seminal Tanjung Sari bungalow garden in Sanur, I borrowed the combination *paras batu* Bali brick wall, which ages beautifully in the Tropics, and the picturesque pixie vale look, done originally by Judith Wawu Runtu-Tumbelaka-Bell and later enhanced by the hand of Donald Friend. I learned to love the humble Hibiscus in all its versions — to this day, common bush variety *Rosa sinensis* is still my favourite. The humble Acalypha also became a friend — so easy to trim and fast to mature. The plant beds in these early testing grounds were big enough to take great swathes of Rhoeo, Wandering Jew and white Agave. I wanted the planting schemes to look like colourful Matisse cutouts from the air. Soon we were creating "window-views" to pagodas, after Capability Brown, and poetically dishevelled water gardens, in the William Kent tradition. But we always worked in the Sanur style: we deferred to the Pandanus, Crinums and sea grape shrubs of the littoral — i.e. the sand dunes along the Sanur coast.

These coastal gardens — the Batu Jimbar estates, the La Taverna and Bali Hyatt hotels and the Bali Oberoi on the West Coast were the testing grounds, if you like, for both the commando squad style of "just do it" garden implementation and the parkland look, bred of my love of the natural English landscape gardens and my love of tropical fecundity. Bill Warren, the Bangkok-based garden writer, called the planting schemes of these early works "imaginative". My Jakarta clients went one step further and said that I "made nothing plants look like something, through unusual combining." The combining grew out of the English tradition of textural contrasts and bright accents (the Codiaeum, white Pampas Grass and *Pistona alba*) and a talent I developed for making tropical naturalism look artful.

Having all these gardens on which to experiment and the willing-and-able Balinese garden-artisans as a talented and vigorous labour force was an ideal way to develop a style, coined "tropical Cotswolds", by the famed garden photographer Tim Street-Porter.

ABOVE: A bird's eye view of the colourful mass plantings of the Bali Hyatt in 1983.

BELOW: The Wantilan Lama garden in Batu Jimbar, a seminal work of the Sanur School.

Chapter 1

A Brief History of Early Tropical Gardens

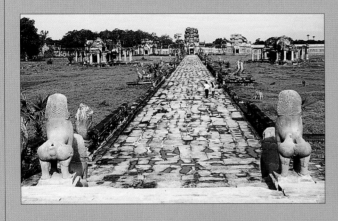  

"*Both urban areas and private gardens planted by Europeans who settled in various colonial possessions drew their inspiration from the remembered landscapes of home, particularly in the use of neatly clipped lawns and tree-lined drives.*"

WILLIAM WARREN, *THE TROPICAL GARDEN*

The history of great tropical parklands visible today follows, for the most part, the history of the Age of Discovery — particularly the history of British colonial expansion (see pages 30–31, A Guide to the Great Colonial Gardens of the Tropical World). The Portuguese left forts, the Spanish left trades and music, but it was the British who left gardens.

Surviving traces of the great landscaped gardens of the ancient tropical world, if we choose to search for them, are few and far between. Only in the avenues of Angkor Thom in Cambodia, and its cousins in Java and Myanmar, do we get any sense of the magnificence of these equatorial "extravaganzas". Time has rendered many others all but unrecognizable.

Two possible exceptions to this rule are the gardens around the tanks at Sigiriya in Sri Lanka and those in the ruins of the Summer Palace of Hue, the Fragrant City, in Central Vietnam. Here one can still find amongst the ruins of the beautifully proportioned courtyards. Decorative Indo-Chinese pagodas, a garden-world alive with ceramic art, ornamental statuary and ancient Plumeria trees can be found. This 19th-century palace garden must have influenced the neighbouring sultans of Java and Sumatra and the rajas of Bali in their ambitious garden-creating. One thinks here of the Chinese rock gardens, called *gunungans*, of the Cirebon and Aceh palaces and the Moorish folly water gardens of the Hamengkubuwono palace in Yogyakarta, Central Java (the core of which dates from the 17th century).

Great tropical botanical gardens followed in the parkland tradition of the Royal Botanic Gardens at Kew and the great English estate parks of the 18th and 19th centuries. One of the first such botanical gardens, established in Sri Lanka, near the ancient hill capital of Kandy, in 1816, remains today as a masterpiece of tropical parkland design — its giant Ficus trees nestle on pastures like small volcanic islands on a placid sea. Rows of exotic Madagascar Fruit de Mer palms are more brazenly beautiful than any avenue or copse at Kew. The Botanic Gardens in St. Vincent, in the West Indies, set into an idyllic valley outside the island capital of Bridgetown, is another natural as well as man-made gem. Surrounded by equatorial rainforest, the St. Vincent gardens feature cannonball trees and the breadfruit made famous by the notorious Captain Bligh, the garden's founder.

The most magnificent tropical botanical garden in Asia today has an interesting history, too. During famed colonial administrator Sir Stamford Raffles' years in Java (1811–16) he invited Kew experts James Hooper and W. Kent to design a botanical garden "like the world had never seen".

The project was eventually instigated by Professor C.G.E. Reinwardt in 1817, after Raffles had moved on to Singapore,

PAGE 22: An early photograph (1890) of the Singapore Botanic Gardens.
PAGE 23, LEFT TO RIGHT: Angkor Wat entrance water garden; the back terrace of the venerable Madras Club in India; the arrival court of the Keraton Kesepuhan in Cirebon, West Java, a rare and exquisite example of Moorish-Chinese colonial tropical palace architecture.
PAGES 24–25: An early 19th-century lithograph of the Dutch colonial town square in Banyu-wangi, East Java.

ABOVE: Nineteenth-century English painter Captain Charles Cazalet's watercolour of a plantation owner's estate on the island of Penang, Malaysia.
OPPOSITE: The water garden Taman Mayura, in Cakranegara, Lombok, Indonesia.
BELOW, RIGHT: An early lithograph of the 14th-century Pura Paibon temple in Banten, an ancient city and sea-port in West Java.
BELOW, LEFT: A 1920s photograph of the palace-fort of the Sultan of Ternate in Maluku (Indonesia's Spice Islands).

with considerable help from the two Kew Gardens experts. Adjacent to the neoclassical palace of the Governor General in Bogor, West Java — itself a wonder of sprawling trees, lakes thick with gleaming water lilies and deer parks — the Bogor gardens grew and grew until they encompassed some two square kilometres (500 acres). Nestled in its bamboo forest at the garden's heart is a rotunda which shelters a monument to Raffles' wife. Bogor has one of the highest annual rainfalls in the world — and two great mountain rivers run through the Kebon Raya botanic garden. The river's valleys are verdant gorges clogged with fern trees and vines. These can be viewed from the long suspension bridges that span between sections of the gardens. The jungle gorges seem impregnable.

Formal water gardens of Taman Raya Bogor feature the mammoth Victoria Regis water lily from South America. Corridors of plantation crops — nutmeg trees, oil palms and cinnamon — remind us that Bogor is also a centre for botanical and zoological research.

The Fairchild Tropical Garden in Miami founded by botanist and philanthropist Captain Montgomery is the 20th-century tropical world's Kew Gardens. Its extensive grounds (larger than Bogor), excellent research facilities and exchange programmes put it leagues ahead of its poorly funded Asian peers with the obvious exception being the spectacular Singapore Botanic Gardens. Both the Fairchild and the Singapore Botanic Gardens feature dense copses of rare palms, which open onto manicured lawns that stretch towards man-made lakes (both gardens sited on former swamp lands). Both have interesting side shows — orchid gardens, spice gardens, Heliconia forests — with well-designed shade structures and paths.

Aesthetically one cannot separate such botanical gardens as these from their dramatic settings. The sub-tropical Sydney Botanic Gardens, for example, have the ravishing harbour; Bogor has its background of volcanic peaks and glistening white colonial buildings; and Peradeniya its views to the most gorgeous rice paddies in the tropical world.

The Madras Club on the Adyar river and the Oranje Club in Batavia (modern day Jakarta) were early tropical pioneers of the neo-European palace in the neo-European parkland look. Perhaps inspired by these vice-regal examples and regal examples like the Mysore Palace in South India, traders and colonial plantation owners from Honolulu to Haiti were, by the end of the 19th century, building haciendas and bungalows with fairly elaborate gardens. In the hills behind Honolulu one finds, still intact, many magnificent gardens from this age. The white portico and the giant shade tree in the front lawn are staples of this plantation house style.

ABOVE, LEFT: Decorative Indo-Chinese planter pots flank the entrance doors to the Saigon Town Hall, Vietnam.
BELOW, LEFT: The quiet high street of a typical 19th-century tropical colonial town.

BELOW, RIGHT: By the late 19th century, neoclassical palaces with substantial English-style parklands, such as this, appeared throughout the tropical world. A driveway sweeps across the lawn.

Lodji Ketjil-Djocja

ABOVE, LEFT: Geoffrey Bawa's tropical-Italianate Lunuganga garden, started in 1950, near Galle, Sri Lanka.

BELOW: Giant Banyan trees line the carriageway to the Sultan's palace in Yogyakarta, Central Java, 1903.

ABOVE: This aerial photograph of the Singapore Botanic Gardens in 1980, shows the floral clock, formal sundial gardens and park beyond. The floral clock was removed in the 1990s by progressive-minded garden trustees.

A Guide to the Great Colonial Gardens of the Tropical World

A tour of the major parklands of the tropical world (modern luxury hotels aside) is essentially a voyage through the history of empire building across the equator during the colonial era. The first stop on such a tropical parkland discovery tour might be the New Oriental Hotel in the fortress town of Galle, on the southern tip of Sri Lanka, the former Ceylon. Here, between superb Portuguese and Dutch colonial buildings dating from the 18th and 19th centuries, one finds palm courts and terrace gardens inspired more by the poetic villa gardens of Sintra outside Lisbon than the extravagant gardens of the Moghul empire in the not-too-distant north. From Galle one should travel on to Peradeniya, Sri Lanka's botanical garden founded by the British colonists in 1816.

The next stop might be the Madras Club in modern Chennai on the East Coast of India where the British East India Company based its trade operations. Here, a handsome white club house with deep terraces and Doric columns overlooks a vast park, built along the lines of the great English parks of the 18th century. Giant canopy trees and woodlands frame a view to the Adyar River, where colonial ladies once genteelly paddled picturesque canoes.

Next visit the island of Banda Neira in the Spice Islands and the former Residence of the Dutch Governor General, another neoclassical architectural gem. Parade grounds lead to the idyllic Banda Harbour which once held the mighty fleet of the Dutch East India Company, the V.O.C.

From here one could side-track to Vietnam and see a more coquettish French entrant in the colonial sweepstakes, the "botanic garden" in Ho Chi Minh City. The quirkish gardens are flanked by the city's Museum of Culture, with buildings in *Indochine* ochre with "empire" frills. Amongst the eccentric chinoiserie of the gardens stand remains of the Peoples' Revolutionary Zoo. Travel north along the coast to Hue, the "Fragrant City" and visit the extensive gardens of the 19th-century Indo-Chinese Summer Palace. From Vietnam one could spend a week exploring the very British Botanic Gardens in Singapore, Bogor (West Java) and Brisbane, Australia. Then head east into the Pacific, to explore the Hawaiian islands — Queen Lili'uokalani's English-tropical park above Honolulu, the treasure-filled Allerton Gardens on the island of Kauai and the breathtakingly romantic Botanic Garden near Hilo, on the Big Island. All these gardens have spectacular locations and wondrous plant collections, particularly palms.

Two other great tropical gardens should be explored in the "New World": the vast Fairchild Botanic Garden in Miami, "The Kew Gardens of the Tropical World" and the piquant botanic garden in St. Vincent, the West Indies, one of the world's oldest, founded in 1814 by Captain Bligh.

ABOVE: The Dutch were very proud of their formal streetscapes in the colonies. This card, dated 1899, shows the town of Pasuruan in East Java. OPPOSITE: The *Victoria amazonica* water lily lake at the Governor General's palace in Bogor, West Java, the home of the tropical world's most abundant botanic garden. RIGHT, TOP TO BOTTOM: Traveller's Palms in a large park in Malaysia; Singapore Botanic Gardens; the very Dutch Pieter Park in Bandung, West Java, exhibits all the busy accents and manicured lawns of European municipal gardens of the 19th century. The Dutch colonial gardens of Indonesia were to bequeath a legacy of municipal streetscaping that haunts much of the archipelago to the present day. Planter boxes with confectionery-type planting were very much a feature of Soeharto's New Order régime.

TROPICAL BUNGALOW GARDENS

"Early Europeans who came to the Tropics had conflicting emotions about their environment. The more romantic were entranced by the splendid luxuriance that surrounded them... Others, probably the majority of those who actually took up residence in such places, found it vaguely threatening: undisciplined and somehow suggestive of a moral laxity. They wanted a more controlled landscape, in part to conjure up nostalgic memories of home but also symbolically to repel the riotous jungle (and possibly riotous natives) that loomed on all sides."

William Warren, *The Tropical Garden*

By the middle of the 19th century, the feisty colonials wanted some glamour in their everyday life. They were tired of stockades and fortresses and life in a plantation hut. They wanted avenues and rows of things, all the same size. They wanted carriageways and gravel drives in which to sweep, back gardens in which to relax and front gardens that displayed status. On the Indonesian island of Banda in the Spice Islands, one still finds rows of neat white neoclassical bungalows sitting in pristine grounds. This neat European-settlement style grew into a sort of tropical "antebellum" formula (great trees, white buildings and rows of palms on sweeping lawns) taken to its apotheosis in the beautiful boulevards of the great trade capitals of the tropical world — Goa, Batavia, Antigua, Caracas, Penang, Madras, Rangoon and Manila. Inland from these coastal capitals, plantation owners turned to estate gardening in the English country house tradition. In the West Indies, one still finds sumptuous estates with rambling tropical gardens. Iris Bannochies' Andromeda estate in Bethsheba, Barbados, is one such fifth-generation Irish-Bajan tropical hybrid. In the Philippines, dynastic families have maintained their magnificent country properties, despite centuries of political change. Sadly, the great Dutch estates of Indonesia and the British estates of Central Africa, Malaysia and tropical India have all but disappeared. Some estates, like the gardens of Queen Lili'uokalani in Honolulu and the colonial mansions of Georgetown, Penang, in Malaysia, survived this epoch of horticultural uncertainty. Others remain as unruly jungles, haunting the suburbs of Colombo, Surabaya and Mozambique.

The graveyard of the colonial settlers on Banda Island is the ultimate "colonial ghost train" garden — eerily beautiful in a uniquely tropical way. This romantic colonial garden style, grown out of the traditions of the great Age of Discovery was, during the first half of 20th century, to influence the last flutter of colonial architects in a profound way. This era of urban expansion (1900–50), when tropical architects were building bungalows for the armed forces and the remaining colonial bureaucrats, was the golden era of the tropical bungalow garden, a hybrid recognized by its blend of English naturalism, Spanish courtyards and Pan-European decorative accents. The combination of architectural elements from indigenous tropical architecture — the wide shady verandah, the elevated platform sleeping quarters, the deep low eaves — and the English love of artful naturalism in a "suburban" setting, blended with over 200 years experience in sweaty climes, gave rise to some truly poetic house and garden settings.

Singapore. European Residence Tanglin.

OPPOSITE, LEFT: Artist Margaret Olley's painting (1956) of a classic Australian "Queenslander" house and garden.
OPPOSITE, RIGHT: A palm and fern garden, in the colonial bungalow style, in a village house in Manado, North Sulawesi, Indonesia.
ABOVE, LEFT: A typical gentleman's bungalow and garden in Singapore, circa 1910. Note the planter pots and Traveller's Palms.
ABOVE, RIGHT: The back verandah and back garden of a plantation owner's house in rural Java in the mid-19th century. Note the rows of ferns in whitewashed planter pots.
TOP: A giant Monkey Pod Tree frames this neat bungalow set in the hills behind Honolulu, Hawaii.

an integral part of Hawaiian design as is a not-inconsiderable Japanese design influence. The cultural diversity of Hawaii — the Chinese, Japanese, Polynesian, Filipino, and East-Coast American missionary influences — is a big part of the Hawaiian Style too and visible in all Hawaiian gardens. There are also the spiky accent plants like Pandanus, giant cacti and the Bromeliads, which don't grow too well in the "real Tropics". The fragrant Plumeria, the Hawaiian "ti" (*Cordyline terminalis*), the creeping ferns and various relatives of the Codiaeum or croton family are also omnipresent. In the late 1960s, Ray Cain of Belt Collins designed a major "lavascape" at the Mauna Lani Resort in Hawaii. Simulated lava rock — used in the construction of waterfalls, lake edges and pavings — is now an essential ingredient for the classic Hawaiian look. The craggy tobacco-brown stone is also a perfect foil for expanses of gleaming lawn.

By the 1970s, the Hawaiian look had invaded every shopping mall from Brisbane to Brasilia. The new growth area for tourism — Southeast Asia — was once again fuelled by Hawaiian experts. The 1970s saw many great Hawaiian hotel gardens by designers like Ray Cain, Jim Nicolay, Bill Bensley, Alan Clarke and Stephen Mechler. In 1979 Belt Collins introduced "Hawaiian Rocks" to Singapore, wrapping a waterfall made from simulated rocks over the Hyatt Regency car park with breathtaking effect.

In 1990, Stephen Mechler and Alan Clarke's Hawaiian garden at the 750-room Grand Hyatt in Nusa Dua Bali, conceived with Balinese firm P.T. Indosekar, stretched garden budgets and neo-Balinese imagination to new heights with sumptuous water courts, sunken gardens and poolscape.

In 1994, Bensley moved from Belt Collins to establish his own studio in Bangkok and develop a highly decorative style renowned for vigorous ethnic artworks and showmanship.

A sprawling Hawaiian-modern tropical garden surrounds this Japanese-style museum building in Honolulu, Hawaii. This tropical Katsura detached palace style, which influenced much of downtown and suburban Honolulu, is one of this century's great tropical design trends.

SUBURBAN GARDENS

The later half of the 20th century has seen a burgeoning in population in nearly all the great tropical cities, and a corresponding interest in gardens in the new suburbs. Schools of tropical design have sprung up — the neo-Hawaiian, the Cocos Island Palm Mall-scape Movement, the Japanese Tropical, the Balinese — to provide comfort and joy for the suburban garden-lover. Many of these "schools" have grown out of the post-colonial naturalist garden movement of the first half of this century; that delightful hybrid of colonial splendour touched upon in Bungalow Gardens (page 32). As average suburban plot sizes have shrunk, from the half acre (0.2 ha) allowed for colonial administrators to the small developers' plots available today — tropical garden design has become focused on swimming pools in backyards, rather than house and garden "duets". Only in the prosperous suburbs of some modern tropical cities does one find gardens of the scale and impressiveness of the beloved old colonial bungalow gardens (see photographs opposite). In garden design one has to be as adept in fashioning art from small, seemingly insignificant spaces (see Small Walled Courts, pages 72–73) as with the larger gardens of the type shown here. As a designer, I "cut my teeth" on glamorous fare — designing, first, a Geoffrey Bawa garden, then the Bali Hyatt, then Peter and Carole Muller's Oberoi — but have since spent most of my career in the suburbs, with the garden lovers, battling it out. It is here that one finds true ism, in both value engineering (i.e. budget management) and garden maintenance.

My advice for smaller gardens is to "have a big idea". Do something bold with the hardscape (pave the lot in red bricks) or water features (do a huge pond with an island) or spend half the budget on a major work of garden art — the plants can follow. Concentrate on the frame (the boundary walls, gates) and the lines (paths, ponds) first, then hide "the uglies" (utility areas, the neighbours), then concentrate on the soft touches.

Lawns tend to be a big part of modern suburban gardens as children love them and they bring a sense of tidiness,

TOP: The gardens of the Residence of the Chinese Ambassador, Honolulu, Hawaii. ABOVE: Adrian Zecha and Ed Tuttle's strict renovation of Geoffrey Bawa's extensions to Donald Friend's garden compound (see image page 47 for the pre-Zecha-Tuttle renovation look). BOTTOM LEFT: Sketch of a garden corner of a house designed by architect Ernesto Bedmar in Singapore.

but they do *look* suburban if small — a paved or swept sand area, for example, looks less "crimped". This book was written for garden lovers on small budgets: I hope that looking through the ideas and images in this book, and more importantly at good gardens in the field, you'll find inspiration and design direction for your contemporary garden. There is a new trend for courtyard style homes (often known as "Bali houses") in suburban areas around the Tropics. These houses often provide internal courtyards to take a more ornamental Oriental look.

TOP: In this garden in Kuala Lumpur, we "borrowed" the neighbours' planting scheme to create an illusion of space. Exposing a stretch of the handsome boundary wall and adding a shapely urn created a pretty vignette.

ABOVE, LEFT: Paul Hutchinson's vibrant garden in northern New South Wales, Australia — wraparound verandahs face a front yard of botanical splendour.

ABOVE, RIGHT: For this house in a suburb of Singapore, I used antique Indian stone columns to create a diversion, or visual barrier, to hide the strident examples of "New Asian" architecture across the way. The lily pond water cascades down stairs and visually joins the swimming pool below.

MODERN TROPICAL GARDENS

classic modern gardens for numerous Scidmore and Owings and Merril-designed buildings in the USA, during the 1950s and 1960s, are note-worthy examples that complement their surroundings — seamless modernity meeting controlled fecundity. My favourites are the stark but shady courts of Geoffrey Bawa's work in Colombo, Sri Lanka, where Pop-Art artifacts are framed by ancient branches; and I admire I.M. Pei's modern "plaza-scapes" in Singapore, where exquisitely-masoned granite slab plazas host towering deciduous trees. These gardens make the spirit soar. The late Brazilian master Roberto Burle-Marx's work throughout the tropical world is anchored in a modernist, almost cubist tradition: Aztec ruinscapes and Amazonian specimens coexist within an atom-age ground plan. His visions are modern, poetic, tropical and romantic. The great Belgian landscaper Jacques Wirtz and many contemporary English landscape designers have had some artistic success with the use of various architectonic forms — either as water bodies, grass mounds or grassy pastures — that act as an arty counterpart to the surrounding leafy countryside. Antonio Gaudi's roofscapes in Barcelona and Debuffet's sculptured garden in the amazing Kruller-Muller sculpture museum in the Netherlands are arguably outdoor works of art and not modern gardens.

In these instances, one may ask, where does modern art stop and gardening begin? There are few good modern sculptors working in tropical parts, so one tends to use primitive art, or large urns, when a striking artwork is needed to balance the composition of a stark courtyard design. "We don't really need a garden", is the *chanson de guerre* so often heard from young designers who think their work is the Getty Museum, Los Angeles. The truth is, only good architecture can support simplicity of surrounds. Most modern architecture looks better with something to soften the façade. Certain plants — bamboos and palms — can look stunning in a modern setting; others, like Hibiscus and Heliconias, tend to look out of place. In tropical houses we also need shade and passive cooling systems — ponds, arbors, terraces — to make a home comfortable. These touches should not be excluded in the name of modernity. Materials like chrome, high-gloss ceramic tiles, and glass balustrades are a challenge in tropical landscape design, and their use in garden areas should be discouraged. The principles of a balanced composition, one that complements the architecture, should be the same whether designing with a modernist or a traditionalist brush.

Designing modern gardens for the Tropics is not always easy — tropical plants have a way of looking old-fashioned. Many of today's bright young architects like to emulate the work of Louis Baragan or Richard Meier, but the "prairie scapes" of this "minimalist" style look sad in the Tropics. Clean, spare lines and glass canopies may be practical for temperate climes where sunlight is often a rare commodity, but anywhere equatorial they leave one moist and sunburnt before reaching the front door.

I believe that the Japanese do the best modern gardens: their spare ancient aesthetic is timeless. In Kyoto, in the many rows of cafes with tiny entrance courts, one will find hundreds of whimsical gardens fashioned from modern materials, such as chain link lamps, bowling ball accents, machine scrubbed marble chips that look both Zen and Zesty. Noguchi's

OPPOSITE: This striking white Art Deco house in Bandung, West Java, has a clever surround — reflecting lake, and anklets of topiary and formal hedges — which complements the striking architecture.

ABOVE, RIGHT: Sri Lankan master designer Geoffrey Bawa does modernism better than anyone else. In this lobby poolscape at the famous Triton Beach Hotel, near Galle, Bawa weaves a "warp" of coloured iron poles and stark Plumeria trunks with a "weft" of grass, polished cement tiles and the swimming pool surface. His modernism is effortless and natural — never clinical.

ABOVE, LEFT: A streetscape in downtown Honolulu, arguably the world's only beautiful modern city. In this photograph, coconut palms are juxtaposed against the handsome lines of a colonial era office block.

RIGHT: A sleek modern internal court in a house and interior which were designed by Geoffrey Bawa in Colombo.

Chapter 2

BALINESE GARDENS

"In creating a Balinese garden one starts with the premise that every piece of land has a spirit and that by 'peopling' the space with plants and ideas one must create absolute beauty in order to placate the spirit."

true Balinese garden is a thing of mystery and romance. "Mysterious" because it poses questions about its inhabitants — the pixies suggested by the ornamental statues, and the spirits who occupy the ubiquitous shrine. "Romantic" because it is in the soul of the Balinese who create gardens to love nature. It is Mother Nature's embracing qualities — Her softness and Her allure that are felt in the Balinese home. This embrace takes in the surrounding architecture and pavilions, all fashioned in fanciful excess, often festooned and framed by plant accessories and accents. The result is mystical and always an exercise in the high art of marrying the natural and the man-made worlds. And, if you're clever, the underworld.

In creating a Balinese garden one starts with the premise that every piece of land has a spirit and that by "peopling" the space with plants and ideas one must create absolute beauty in order to placate the spirit.

Restless artists feel an overpowering sense of joy and tranquillity when presented with a Balinese courtyard in full ceremonial flush — its decorations so beautiful and its inhabitants so picturesque. Likewise a well-composed Balinese garden — with a balance of the fecund, the ornamental and the mystical — allows its admirer a sense of well-being or oneness with nature. Far-fetched? Well, I've watched bankers and even developers go weak at the knees and wet around the edges, when led into a fully flourishing Balinese garden like the fern court of the Bali Hyatt at Sanur or the Jagat Nata temple at Ketewel village with its tortured Plumeria and ancient pagodas. How do mere mortals make Balinese gardens, is the question, when it seems to require Merlin's craft.

"Is it possible to have a Balinese garden without having a Balinese house?" is another interesting question that springs to mind.

The essence of a Balinese garden is artful naturalism with ornamentation — the "peopling" of a space with sensual (well, curvaceous) silhouettes and shrines or statues or pots nuzzling up to trees. The sense of creative maintenance — the draping of delicate vines, the applying of orchids to trees and the hanging of birdcages — is an important characteristic. The presence of adjacent terraces or pavilion spaces is another essential ingredient.

A Balinese garden, like a Japanese garden, is designed to be viewed from a low-eaved pavilion but is, traditionally, more of a work horse than an aesthetic marvel. Even temple courts, like the water gardens of the Kesiman Palace or the "floating" temple Taman Ayun on a man-made lake at Mengwi, are designed more for practicality than for picturesqueness. A Balinese garden is to be traversed: the courtyard floor is either swept dirt or red brick and, only recently, with the advent of the

ABOVE: Donald Friend's 1973 painting of Chris Carlisle's beachside bungalow and garden in Batujimbar, Sanur.

OPPOSITE: Brent Hesselyn and Wayan "Braggie" Latra created this beautiful garden at the Taman Mertasari near Sanur, Bali. This house and garden inspired many early Sanur developments.

PAGE 42: Belgian painter Le Mayeur's muse,

Ni Pollock, in their idyllic Balinese garden on the beach in Sanur, Bali.

PAGE 43, LEFT TO RIGHT: Rustic Balinese gate and entrance pond at Walter Folle's house at Ubud, Bali, 1979; Majapahit era (1600–1800) red-brick Balinese temple; a corner of the pool gardens at the Amandari hotel near Ubud, Bali; the Bali Hyatt Sanur gardens painted by Sakiko Ibuchi.

PAGE 44–45: Entrance pond at the Villa Bebek.

The garden at right was created over five years. It took that long for the central tree to reach the right size to balance the composition. The charm is found in the way this tree dissects the off-verandah view into two complementary halves — one bushy and "in one's face", the other mysterious, snaking off towards infinity. Water gardens are best placed to be viewed with the sun either rising or setting over them. The low afternoon light in this photograph illuminates the magentas and shrieking canary yellows. Artworks variously nestle and direct, as the eye searches for a way out.

Japanese artist Sakiko Ibuchi's painting of the full-fauvist Bali Hyatt gardens captures the three essential elements of a Balinese garden — fecundity, ornamental accents and Balinese activity.

THE RUSTIC CHARM MOVEMENT

TOP: Cacti by the dusty wall of a Balinese pondok.

ABOVE: Water lilies in a rustic Balinese trough.

OPPOSITE: Entrance porch and garden of the Amanbrioche Cottage, the Taman Bebek Hotel, Sayan, Bali – a real rustic charmer.

BELOW: Batik-dyeing urn, the Big Bamboo compound, Bali.

The Rustic Charm Movement of garden design was founded in the early throes of the 20th century. It was perhaps then that the more artistic Dutch settlers on Bali rejected the herbaceous borders of their homeland and went, instead, for garden planning of a native Balinese style — a plot of swept dirt, a scattering of palms, and some colourful freestanding shrubs.

It was in the hills of Ubud, however, some fifty years later that the Rustic Charm Movement really took root — in the mud wall and statue gardens of European artists like Rudolf Bonnet and Hans Snell, who both spent much of their adult lives in mossy Balinese villages, absorbing beauty. Their gardens inspired a young Australian poet, John Darling, who was living in the rice fields north of the town (see page 21). His first bamboo *pondok* had an Hibiscus hedge boundary fence, a quaint lily pond with island shrine, built in the Zen-like style of the high mountain villages he so admired, and a cow in a manger. He carved a little path in the nearby ravine's side, that led to a spring below, and asked his friend, artist Wayan Cemul, to carve a few anthropomorphic planter pots to "people" the walk. Cemul pots now "people" hotels all over the world.

A decade passed, and John Darling's charmingly rustic garden slowly expanded to include new courtyards, with bamboo gates and terraces and platform mounds (locally called *compang*, see pages 188–189) of the Neolithic-style raised platforms one finds in many of Bali's more ancient villages.

My own mud-walled studio-home in Sanur, built during 1979–84 (see photo page 20), was inspired by John Darling's house and garden. It was here that I first used a soapstone water vat, called a *lesung*, as a trough for my Japanese-style *mandi* bathroom. To look authentic, a Balinese "rustic-charm" garden must remain true to the minimalist aesthetic spirit of "mountain Bali", but not go overboard in a "Fred Flinstone, Barney Rubble" direction. Heaven forbid!

In planning a "rustic-charm" garden, choose a corner of your garden that is essentially Balinese — that is, a quiet corner or courtyard. If there is a boundary or a building wall adjacent, it should be finished with a rustic treatment. Thatch-topped packed mud is the Rolls Royce of such garden walls but bamboo, rubble or moss-covered brick can be just as effective. Artwork accents should be chosen or designed for their simplicity. For example, a stone lantern or shrine should be pre-Hindu. Planting schemes should look natural and be taken from a palette of rural Balinese plants such as sugar cane, bananas, tree ferns or kitchen herbs. Ground covers look better than grass; swept dirt or cobblestones look best of all.

Creating any garden can be an exercise in fantasy and folly. Starting with a gentle aesthetic is a good way to develop your own original garden style.

Chapter 3

COURTYARDS, PATIOS, TERRACES AND WALLED COMPOUNDS

"*The courtyard garden — called* tsuboniwa *in Japanese — is a garden in a small, enclosed area. The gardener does not fill it up; this would only congest it. Instead he carefully arranges a few items and uses their relationship to suggest more than is immediately visible to the eye.*"

KIYOSHI SEIKI, *A JAPANESE TOUCH FOR YOUR GARDEN*

f, as is widely believed, patios were the gift of the Arab world to Mediterranean architecture, then courtyard architecture — sometimes called pavilion style — is the East's gift to the Tropics. The tropical adaptation of traditional Chinese and Japanese courtyard architecture has bequeathed a world of wonders. The notion of having a garden which can be viewed from its four sides and having a garden design that is simultaneously an outdoor living area and a thing of beauty, is integral to the design philosophy of Arab, Persian, Indian and Southeast Asian architecture.

In the Tropics, particularly in Bali and Thailand, where the classic walled compound consists of interlocking garden courts and scattered pavilions, the garden enthusiast has maybe 10 or 20 "canvases" on which to work. Balinese, Thai and Cambodian temples provide formal references on a far grander scale for the aesthetic concepts of courtyard architectural style.

The much-lauded Franco-Vietnamese film *The Scent of Green Papaya* (1984) showcased the magic and mystery of the tropical courtyard home. From the film one remembers the raindrops falling heavily from the low-slung eaves, the luminescent greens of papaya and banana leaves catching the strong shafts of tropical light, and an atmosphere portrayed of a courtyard house that is a chequer-board of alternating open and semi-closed spaces.

Anyone who has ever walked the tight lanes of Bangkok, Ho Chi Minh City or Yogyakarta knows the feeling. Narrow house gates or noodle shop fronts lead into tranquil oases of verdant foliage, carved colonnades, covered walkways, and pond-side pavilions. In Manila, the Intramuros district of the old city creates a Moorish-Spanish version of the same phenomenon. It evokes an atmosphere that was once unique to tropical Asian dwellings, but which is now much copied around the tropical world — from the Caribbean to the Congo.

My first courtyard garden, in fact my first garden ever, was in the subtropical reaches of Glebe, Sydney's university suburb. I was an architecture student and had long admired the perfection of the universes-in-miniature created by Japanese garden designers. In the shell of a burnt-out terrace house I created a clumsy moss garden, "after Ryo-anji", a neo-Balinese temple court, and a "sliver garden", off a long terrace, that featured a 15-metre-long (12-foot-long) Hokusai wave painted on a corrugated iron fence. Part of the house was also the venue for weekly meetings of the Glebe Women's Filmmaker Collective who would regularly scold me, as they refused to slip off their massive cork-heeled mules, with taunts of, "Whaddya think this is — China or something?"

I have never looked back. Doing small courts is still my pride and joy.

PAGE 56: The central "patio" courtyard in architect Geoffrey Bawa's house in Colombo, Sri Lanka.

PAGE 57, LEFT TO RIGHT: In a very small bathroom garden, designed for a Jakarta house in 1996, I used an old molasses-boiling vat as a central artwork, filled with dwarf water lilies. On the wall I placed an Asmat shield and a small square of soapstone carving, in the Majapahit style. The slate skirting was inspired by farmhouse walls I had seen in Yunnan, South China; a path across the sand court of the Villa Bebek, Sanur, Bali; the water court and terraced gardens of

a boutique hotel called Puri Canggu Mertha, designed by our office in 1998.

PAGES 58–59: Tim Street-Porter's stunning photo of the arrival pond at the Amandari, Bali in the first year of its inception.

TOP: A 19th-century print of a Fijian village.

ABOVE: My first courtyard garden in Glebe, Sydney, Australia.

OPPOSITE: "Coral garden" at the Bali Hyatt, Sanur, Bali. See also page 63.

*Family planning statuettes
gaze out of a window at
the tightly interlocking
courts of the Villa Bebek.*

*The inner sanctum of
gentleman aesthete K.R.T.
Hardjonegoro (Go Tik Swan)
in the old Central Javanese
capital of Surakarta. Pink
Plumerii, Vietnamese pots and
Chinese bird cages are an
inspired counterpoint to the
masculine lines of the Art
Deco house and furniture.*

Now, there are many different courtyard garden styles. There are walled-in courts, such as those found in tropical bathroom gardens. (Australian architect Peter Muller's famous Bali Oberoi bathroom has been much copied.) There are entrance courts, with paths or stepping stones across them, and central courts which are "internal islands" to be viewed while perambulating around colonnades. There are sculpture courts, fern courts, palm courts and auto courts for cars.

The garden space in traditional Southeast Asian courtyards is often "peopled" with statues and shrines, and shaded by small-leaved fruit trees, such as Star Fruit or Guava. As home courtyards are used for milling about, cleaning one's bicycle or, occasionally, for dance performances and wedding feasts, part of the floor is often paved, or compacted, with regular sweeping, into a hard earthen mass. Orchids, epiphytes, bird cages and pergolas enhance the "Oriental ornamental" look.

In the ancient communities of tropical Asia, the whole village is designed along the courtyard architectural principle. The main square or central alleyway is everyone's open sitting room. Longhouses or communal pavilions run along the central axis which is often terraced into different courts defining different status.

During the age of trade, when Indian and Chinese cultural models were first introduced, the tropical Asian village took on a less linear form with the villages and the houses becoming more cruciform. Courtyards became more boxlike with pavilions arranged around a central court. Palaces became multi-courtyard labyrinths with pleasure gardens in the prevailing popular "Chinese mountain", "Moghul-style" floating pavilion or European folly style. Some of these gardens and many ancient temples survive today to inspire courtyard garden enthusiasts.

ABOVE: Entrance court in black candi stone (andesite) at the main dining room of the Four Seasons Resort, Jimbaran, Bali.

LEFT: The "Coral Garden" court of the Bali Hyatt, photographed ten years after the picture on page 60.

TERRACES AND PATIOS

Helen Von Bueren reclines in a Thai pavilion, called a sala, *in her dramatic Bangkok house compound. The* Lanna Thai *temple drum and mature Traveller's Palms help form a "walled" or "screened" court off one side of the pavilion. Other sides lead to deep vistas and a central courtyard area of lawn.*

PAGES 64–65: A leafy terrace garden in a country setting in Hawaii. The scattering of rare plants in pots, even on the table, creates a homely feel that suggests both avid gardener and pot collector.

RIGHT: Entrance court designed by Oliver Messel for Clonsilla, Lady Honour Guinness's house in Mustique.

Well-designed tropical houses have climate-friendly verandahs or terraces on which to pick up a passing breeze. These terraces are often decorated with potted plants and comfortable furniture from which to survey a garden view. Patios, or outdoor courts, whether surrounded on all sides or just open to the sky like an outdoor terrace, are a useful addition to any tropical house where night-time entertaining can take place under the stars.

The architecture of arid Middle Eastern cities is laden with built-in roof terraces and patios sparkling with fountains. Tropical houses, by contrast, tend to grow outdoor decks or garden terraces as usage patterns and favourite views become apparent. Decorating a friendly patio or terrace is an art in itself. They look best with furniture and potted plants "casually collected" in a mixture of shapes and sizes (see pages 176–177). Fixed outdoor tables can be used for potting or flower arranging, spread with cactus collections and waterproof lamps to create a "lived in" look. Side tables of stone are practical too, and can grow beards of ferns and epiphytes during the wet season. The best patio paving is simple — Roman brick or other handmade or hand-chiselled natural stone. Remember the drainage when planning a patio and the plumbing if you want a decorative water feature. I find the current trend for pebble aggregate and other nature-alienating finishes abhorrent. Think of Victorian paved gardens and the soft pelt growth fresh moss brings.

Terraces and patios look more dramatic with a tree. In Arab countries the "interference element" is often a lime tree; in the Tropics a palm or a plumeria may provide vertical relief. Ponds in the centre of a patio and at the side of a terrace are excellent passive cooling systems and they provide visual interest, particularly when lit properly at night.

This "patio" style courtyard in a Manila suburban house uses a plethora of strong decorative elements — central dry pond, bonsai accent, rustic arch, mossy pavers — within a palm and bamboo jungle court.

Bamboo or timber decks are a pleasant addition to any tropical house — they provide eyries from which to survey, and cool, shady corners if wrapped around trees, like this example. In this Filipino country house, wraparound benches have been added onto the railing — they are unpretentious and practical.

SMALL WALLED COURTS

ABOVE: Japanese in scale, with tropical intensity and Javanese decorative elements — a small garden in the Balinese home of interior decorator Hinke Zieck.

RIGHT: My office worked with Indonesian architect Tan Tjiang Ay on the Harmoko house in Jakarta in 1985. The architect allowed us to create an arrival experience that was dramatic and Oriental, to go with the "Han farm house" lines of the house. We decorated both architecture and interior space to get our desired garden look.

OPPOSITE: I designed a "living room built into the side of a hill" for a Singapore client in 1990. Two "sunken courtyards" grew out of the architectural design, which we treated in a formal almost modern way using rare palms in a graded pebble court. A limestone planter pot-cum-light, by Wayan Cemul of Bali, is visible in the top left hand corner of the photograph.

"The word 'paradise' is derived from the old Persian word pairidaeza, *which means enclosed garden."*

Tan Hock Beng, *Tropical Architecture and Interiors*

When designing gardens for private homes I am often presented with the problem of how to enhance a long narrow space viewed from an interior room or terrace. Usually, I expose a section of wall and let the narrow space "bleed out" a bit, over the top of the wall. A sense of unravelling layers and, somehow, space is achieved as the eye tells the heart to be comforted by this "outlook". A well-designed small courtyard can be like an opera set by Watteau or a pre-Raphaelite painting. The proximity and the scale allow for appreciation of even the tiniest detail.

The photographs on these two pages demonstrate the agreeable "picture" presented by a small but well-designed courtyard garden. The hardscape (steps, walls, pebbles), softscape (the plants) and accents (artwork) are well balanced, and tufts of wispy planting in the foreground soften the viewing frame of the composition.

Sand, pebbles and small-leafed ground covers look best on the floor of small courts, in combination with plants that are statuesque or striking, like papyrus, palm or ferns. The delicacy of the planting scheme thus contrasts, in a pleasing way, with the harder character of the surrounding walls.

Just remember — small is beautiful.

VILLA BEBEK COURTS

ABOVE: *I set this gate into a dense grove of Alexandra Palms and yucca-like* Cordyline invisa. *The gate was inspired by traditional Balinese village house gates.*

RIGHT: *A lunch spot looks through a "window" in the planting, across the pool, to an ornamental gate in the far courtyard wall. In the foreground are a cast-iron Victorian plant stand, wall-tap gargoyles and carved wall panels.*

OPPOSITE: *The staff kitchen of the P.T. Wijaya offices at the Villa Bebek features a raised dining area surrounded by classical Balinese statuary. I used "majorelle blue" powder from Morocco to add "jump" to the end wall.*

The Villa Bebek in Sanur, Bali is a house of over fifty courtyards — small walled and otherwise. Some twenty of these courtyards are presented in the pages of this book, in photographs taken over a period of five years. A brief look at Atang Fachruroji's aerial view drawing of the compound will give the reader an overview of this courtyard complex (see Appendix, page 198).

The ten buildings of the compound are intricately interlocked through a network of gates and courtyards and garden walls. Ponds assist in providing privacy or at least act as barriers to keep the adjoining villa's dog out! Each of the tropical pavilions opens onto garden terraces on at least two of its sides. These terraces are linked through a complex labyrinth of paths, ponds, pergolas and internal Balinese gateways.

In 1997, I pulled down the walls separating the three villas of the property and redesigned the gardens. The Villa Bebek then entered a new phase as a studio-home and testing ground for garden design ideas. As tropical gardens are such fun to rearrange, the Villa Bebek grounds have monthly overhauls whenever an inspiring new light or planter arrives.

It is a peaceful garden oasis amidst the urban sprawl of present-day Sanur.

ABOVE: The path from the "blue room" passes through a Balinese courtyard garden, and one of the house shrines. I used a bright tropical palette and lots of ferns, philodendrons and flowering vines to contrast with the simplicity of the "coastal court" opposite (see right).

RIGHT: View from the washbasin over the small courtyard garden. From the loo one spies the "blue majorelle" Moroccan feature-niche with its soapstone statue.

A Small Court in the Coastal Tradition

This small court, off the blue "Moroccan" room in the Villa Bebek (see plan, opposite), was created in the pre-Hindu *pesisir* or Balinese coastal culture style. As it is a tight space sharing a boundary with a dense palm grove, I chose white sand, white-washed walls and white cacti as the main ingredients. Two small niches in the high Atlas (Berber) style of Morocco were carved out of the courtyard wall either side of the bed and painted "majorelle" (cobalt) blue, to effect a "leaching" out from the interior design character.

A lamp inspired by a Sumatran Batak stool, and an antique carved stone panel from a high mountain village in Bali set in the wall, were added as strikingly simple accents. The court is viewed from three rooms and also acts as a private yard for the bedroom. Limestone stepping stones on the white-sand courtyard floor act as demarcators, indicating to guests that they may enter or exit the bedroom via either of the courts if they wish.

Reticence in softscape (the "growies", or plants) is important in creating small courts in the Tropics. The treatment of the courtyard and the house wall, the choice of paving materials, and the addition of artwork accents and the lighting are also important in achieving a harmonious composition. Use statues or ornamental plants like cacti, Crinums and handsome stands of palms. Ferns, Rhoeo and Mondo Grass are very useful ground covers in small courts of this style.

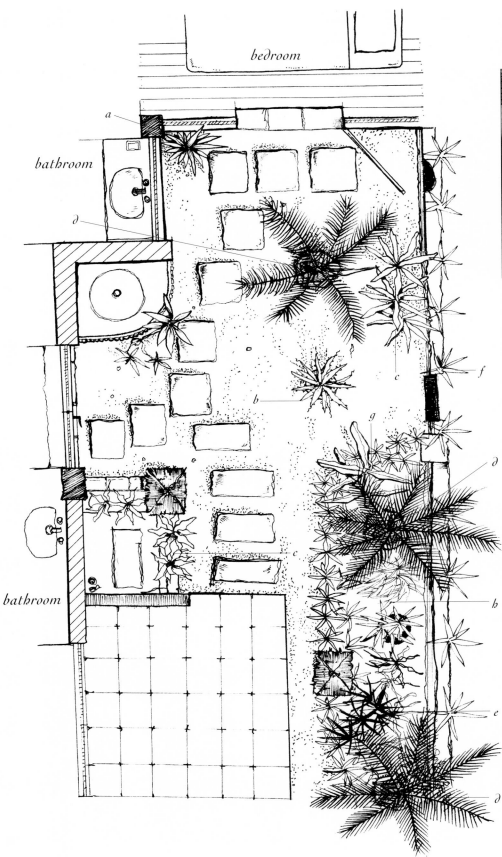

bedroom

bathroom

bathroom

a

∂

b

c

f

g

∂

h

e

∂

*The view to the southern
"coastal" court
from the blue room.*

*Planting plan for the
"coastal" court:*
a. Cordyline terminalis
b. Aloe vera
c. Rhoeo spathacea
∂. Cocos nucifera
e. Rhapis humilis
f. Purpia agave
g. Alpinia purpurata
h. Arundo donax
    versi color

Fig a

Fig b

Fig c

Fig ∂

Fig e

Fig f

Fig a: A pedestal pot of Aloe vera *(used for sunburn relief)* is a striking accent in the daytime and a garden light at night. The base is a hollow fibreglass mould taken from a North-Sumatran Batak stool with a waterproof bollard light underneath.

Fig b: View of the courtyard from the bed in the blue room.

Fig c: A Japanese-style garden fence shields the unsightly hot-water system. It is constructed of bamboo, split bamboo and sugar-palm fibre (ijuk) string.

Fig ∂: The Berber niche with a High Atlas (Moroccan) soapstone statue. The cactus growing on the wall acts to enforce security.

Fig e: Above the courtyard a winged lion keeps guard.

Fig f: A detail of the pitted soapstone (paras batu) enclosure which hides the air-conditioning compressor from view, without impeding its air flow.

PATHS AND PAVINGS

This 'break out zone' of a broad terrace of a large living room in a big modern Singapore house needed special treatment. The paving mix I chose — pebbles and grey slate pavers — is neutral enough not to distract from the "big story" (the magnificent tree and nestling water lily vat) but "smart" enough to create a sense of enclosed court, which is appealing.

Leaf imprinting cement pavers is a clever way to "soften" a hardscape.

Many good gardens have been ruined by "overzealous" paving — either too stiff or too shiny. The old Getty Museum in Malibu, California, with its aggressive wheelchair compatibility and the revamped Raffles Hotel in Singapore are two examples. Compare the footpaths of Orchard Road, Singapore, designed to withstand a nuclear winter, with the cobbled streets of ancient Roman towns like Cordoba, Spain, or even Paris. If landscaping is the camouflage for bad architecture then paranoid or ostentatious paving is the Achilles' heel of many landscapers.

In Europe, garden lovers get misty-eyed over the first brick paver from Byzantium — whole gardens are created in the cracks in pavings. In tropical gardening, however, one cannot afford to be too "soft" — sodden turf and muddy patches are the bane of tropical courtyards. Pavers and pebbles of some sort are quite often a necessity. The trick is to make them look like a luxury.

After a heavy rain, stepping stones are needed in all but the best-drained gardens. Care should be taken when designing small walled courts, in particular, as it can take a while for the sodden conditions to disappear.

In most courtyard situations there is not enough space or light for grass to grow well — and turf quickly turns muddy if frequently traversed. Using rustic porous materials for pavers encourages the growth of moss, which is a mixed blessing. While adding that desired "patina", moss also spells trouble on a stair tread or courtyard floor. One should avoid highly polished surfaces outdoors — they get slippery and dangerous with a light rain too. Choose a paving material that matches both budget and the garden character: swept earth or white sand look brilliant in palm groves, for example and terracotta bricks are perfect for fern courts. Limestone pavers are good by the pool. I often use brick or natural-stone pavers, preferably with a bush hammer or "split" finish, as uneven edges look better in nature.

The choice of paver has a big influence on the courtyard garden's composition. If there's already a lot of "jump" in your garden — colour, furniture, birdcages — and there is a risk that the space may feel confined, match the courtyard paver with architectural floor finishes of verandahs, pavilions or rooms adjoining the garden spaces. If the gardens need a lift, introduce a bold pattern in the paving, or a weave pattern, or a fancy grout.

Remember that a fully paved surface sends torrential rainwater off in sheets, so it will need to be quickly collected, somewhere, and dispensed with. Holes in the paving scheme with trees in them are always a good idea in the Tropics: they allow water to soak away and also provide "vertical relief" — as architects love to call trees near buildings. Trees provide shade for garden-dwellers, a play of shadows on the pavement and strong sculptural form — an intrusive element in the view.

Avoid hard edges, such as curbs on planting beds or borders in the paving pattern, as too many strong lines upset the "artful naturalism". Choose materials that age gracefully and provide "supporting role" backup to the "stars" of the courtyard — the steps, statues and planter pots.

All terracotta landscape schemes look wonderful in the Tropics, and certainly have been much used here throughout history. White on white garden schemes — such as limestone pavers and white sand, with whitewashed walls and white flowering plants — look great in a coastal location. Dark grey stones (granite, andesite) give a cool, handsome look and, if porous, act to cool passively when wet. Grey stone looks particularly good next to grass, if you don't want the "sporty" look that white borders and accents give.

And then there are outdoor cement finishes — the good old cement pavers with pebbles set into the grout, and the leaf imprint pavers popularized by legendary Sri Lankan architect Geoffrey Bawa. Hexagonal pavers are good because they allow an "organic" line when joined in a line or shape.

Pebbles, spread thinly on a brick base or thin concrete slab, make for a clean spacious look. They provide good surface drainage and are very useful in the zone under the eave where ground covers tend not to grow. Without some treatment in this zone mud is often adjacent to the pavilion or terrace floor.

Paving slabs or tiles set like stepping stones in a court of pebbles, with ground covers, shrubs and trees used sparingly, can create an interesting Oriental look for any small garden space. Such pathways can give a sense of passage — a dynamic edge — to an otherwise static garden space.

ABOVE: Harlequin pattern pavers on the fourth-floor roof garden of the Grand Hyatt, Singapore.

BELOW, LEFT TO RIGHT: Go Tik Swan's "imperial-sixties" masterpiece garden in his Central Javanese town house features simple andesite pavers with a stark white grout; limestone pavers in grey pebbles look "sporty" and bring "definition" to an entrance court; hexagonal pavers allow one to have organic lines where the path meets the garden or grass.

n

o

Garden designers must learn to love stone and understand the cut, colour, and laying pattern of different types. Pictured are examples of attractive uses:
(a) slate squares (30 x 30 x 3cm) embedded in earth in a circular pattern ; (b) granite pieces laid in a "crazy" pattern in a cement and clay mix; (c) similar to "b" but a less "crazy" pattern; (d) limestone pavers (50 x 50cm) on compacted sand bed in a chequered pattern with couch grass in between;
(e) slate squares (25 x 2cm) on compacted sand with a 5cm grass "grout"; (f) square bricks (15 x 15 x 8cm) butt-jointed (no grout) on compacted sand; (g) cobble-stones in three colours laid in a Chinese wall pattern on cement; (h) rough house bricks on com-pacted sand and soil; (i) basket-weave pattern of granite bricks (11 x 12 x 8cm); (j) washes of sorted (3–5cm) river pebbles laid in a sand and cement base; (k) slate and pebble pattern; (l) West Javan lime-stone (maximum 100cm long) laid in a "crazy" pattern on concrete with white grout; (m) "Copacabana" pattern using lozenge-shaped pavers and white grout;
(n) concrete triangles (20 x 8cm) laid in grass, following a Nepalese paving pattern; (o) split granite pavers (30 x 40 x 6cm) set in grass in a random parallel pattern; (p) pebbles in a sandy clay and soil mix which allows fine grass to grow through (micro-maintenance required); (q) Portuguese roof tiles (side on) form this tight mixed-pebble pattern; (r) another striking pebble pattern; (s) marble and quartz chips in a decorative medallion in a house's porch.

STEPS

Ancient villages in the Pacific often have stone ramps and not steps. This Bali Aga village house gate in Tenganan, East Bali, is reached via a handsome river stone ramp.

BELOW, LEFT TO RIGHT: A landing in the garden of the Taman Bebek Hotel, near Ubud, Bali becomes a vestibule of interest with the addition of ornamental elements; the stair itself can be a work of art; the coral stairs set into the coral cliffs of the Four Seasons Resort, Jimbaran's foreshore parklands. Note the teak tree branch balustrade that complements the rustic look of the outdoor staircase.

"Steps are the unsung heroes of architectural design. One always thinks of the towering gate rather than the magnificent flight of steps leading to it. Or the handsome pavilion rather than the elegantly proportioned, tiered base. Steps are the grandstands of Balinese courtyard theatre, and the spare seats of a thousand banquets. Steps are for scraping thongs on in the wet season, for sunning prawn crackers in the dry, and for kicking dogs down after a bad hand of dominoes."

Made Wijaya, *Balinese Architecture*

An ordinary backyard can become a place of interest and romance with the imaginative addition of a few changes of level. Ten thousand London "Chelsea backyards" teach us that terracing courtyard space creates garden "rooms" which can be decorated individually. A handsome flight of stairs (see photo opposite) can become a work of art and help orient a garden user to the main views: many garden designers create major vistas from the top of a flight of stairs, or from the break in a hedge "fortified" by a change in level.

Rough-hewn stone is best for the garden steps in a natural garden. However care should be taken in the Tropics to ensure that the chosen stone doesn't get too mossy in the wet season. The treatment of the relationship between the tread (depth) and the rise (height) of the flight of steps and the surrounding setting is of prime importance in good garden step design. Too many hard edges or contrasting materials results in what I call "racing stripes" in nature. In most cases, the bigger the stone slabs are the better a set of steps looks. A thicker more rustic rise is a good rule of thumb, too.

ABOVE: A French artist's charming watercolour of the entrance to the Taman Bebek hotel in Bali.

LEFT: This house in Calatagan, the Philippines, uses small-scale stones to create a dramatic artwork, perhaps inspired by the staircases in old Spanish citadels, that leads down and into a Zen spiral sand garden. The view and the rustic architecture complete a picture of sublime original beauty.

The main dining room of the Four Seasons Resort in Bali is modelled on a Balinese water palace. At the end of a series of ponds and colonnades the main kitchen wall backs onto the water garden. The architects, Martin Grounds and Jack Kent, allowed me to dress up the wall and create a sort of 'faux-entrance' to the fictitious Raja's private pavilion. Luckily a gorgeous North Bali palace door with matching windows was on the market. We snapped it up and set it into a "veneer" wall of soapstone which now, some eight years later, exudes the "kiss of centuries" look so easy to achieve in tropical garden design. Large limestone pavers and simple papyrus, water lily and bulrush plants, placed sparingly, complete the pretty picture.

Chapter 4

WATER GARDENS

"*Water was the element which made the creation of the garden possible;*
in various manifestations throughout the history of garden design,
it has continued to provide essential life and interest."

GEORGE PLUMPTRE, *THE WATER GARDEN*

he most perfect tropical garden is Pura Luhur temple at Uluwatu in Bali, a marvel of coral shrines and pagodas perched on a narrow promontory 200 metres (660 feet) above the pounding waves of the Indian Ocean. If, as the English say, the ideal garden is a mixture of the natural and the man-made then this spectacular work of art created by the 15th-century priest and architect Dwijendra, is surely a masterpiece.

Traditional Chinese landscape designers talk about the importance of balancing of the *shan* (mountain) and the *shui* (sea). The ancient Indian and Japanese garden architects, similarly, tried to create perfect microcosms symbolizing the holy mount of Mahameru "floating" on the eternal ocean.

Across Southeast Asia, palace architecture employs formal and informal bodies of water in the "pleasure courts". The imperial gardens in Hue, Central Vietnam, the Taman Sari water palace in Yogyakarta, Central Java and the water follies of the kings of East Bali and West Lombok (Tirta Gangga, Taman Ujung, Taman Narmada and Taman Mayura) are all royal water gardens influenced by both Eastern and Western traditions of beauty and cosmogony, with a healthy dose of tropical ornamentation in the choice of plants and trees.

On a more mundane level many of us are drawn to the beauty of the oceans and mountain lakes with their vast expanses of blue, and their shifts of light both subtle and dramatic. Water reflects. Water cools.

Most of the great tropical gardens of the world incorporate bodies of water and water features to some extent. We find water tanks, reflecting ponds and moats in the ancient Persian-Moghul tradition. In the gardens of the European colonialists one finds lakes and ponds either in water gardens, elaborately planted in the grand English tradition, or formal reflecting bodies in the classic French mode. The garden at Lunuganga, Geoffrey Bawa's English-Italianate home near Galle in Sri Lanka, is a series of terraces and fields that fold and step down to a vast lake, the backdrop for all his loosely controlled views.

More common in the tropical world, particularly in Asia, are water gardens that exist between buildings as rectilinear bodies of water in courtyard confines. In Angkor Thom, the ancient city to the north of the legendary Angkor Wat, I discovered an 11th century swimming pool with a laterite block edge of cascading steps. Among the city's ruins are many charming water temples of which Angkor Wat itself is the most remarkable. The old palace at Mandalay also featured a stepped-edge tank surrounded by fairy-tale colonnades. The Moghul palaces at Goa, indeed many of the Moghul palaces of India, use ghats, artificial lakes and reflecting ponds as foils in courts adjoining their gleaming palaces and mausolea.

PAGE 90: The Chinese water garden at the Bali Hyatt hotel, Sanur.

PAGE 91, LEFT TO RIGHT: The entrance pond at Geoffrey Bawa's Triton Beach Hotel in Sri Lanka;

a Balinese water temple; publisher Hans Höfer's koi pond in Singapore.

PAGES 92–95: The entrance water garden at the Four Seasons Resort, Jimbaran, Bali.

OPPOSITE: Granite paving stones frame a small water garden in a courtyard near Manila, the Philippines.

ABOVE, TOP TO BOTTOM: A traditional tank near a mosque in Sumatra; the King of East Bali's 1940 water garden folly, Tirta Gangga; poolside at the Von Bueren's house in Bangkok.

In the tight courtyards of Thailand's traditional architecture, bodies of water, either moving *klong* (canals) or lotus ponds, are as integral to the architecture as the fabric of the buildings themselves. In coastal Hawaiian gardens, there is often a natural lava rock alive with coral fish, if saltwater; or with water lilies, if freshwater. One thinks here of Brother Foster's enchanting retreat on the Kona coast, on Hawaii, built around a 2-hectare (5-acre) aquatic park of such rock pools. In the 19th century, on neighbouring Oahu, Queen Lili'uokalani built a vast garden in the lush hills above Honolulu, with a legendary swimming-hole fed by a cascading waterfall — the Rolls Royce of tropical water features. Indeed waterfalls and cascades, man-made and natural, provide the greatest delight in the garden design world. If large enough they have an ionizing effect on the air, which can move enchantment to intoxicating levels.

In the tropical reaches of Mexico, in the regions where the ancient Mayan civilization once thrived, one finds incredible sunken waterholes, called *ceynotes*, of great clarity and natural beauty, brimming water lilies and iris. These *ceynotes*, most often found adjacent Mayan temples, had a macabre use, too — as aquatic graves for human sacrifices!

In present-day Bali, the "poodle in puddle" look (the barely floating pavilions found in expatriate dream homes) has become synonymous with the architecture of the tourist boom. During the 1990s, swimming pools, likewise, became more about architectural impact and less about swimming. But the tourist meccas of the tropical world — Acapulco, Bali and Hawaii — continue to produce heavenly water gardens and aquatic theme parks.

As this book is concerned primarily with romantic tropical gardens, I will not touch on the broader discussion of trends in modern tourism design nor on charming backyard waterfalls and cascades — both subjects covered in many other learned books. I will concentrate in this chapter on my love for water spouts, bird baths, lotus ponds and mountain spas, and try to show you how to create poetic water gardens and romantic bathing pools.

The entrance court in black candi stone (andesite) at the main dining room of the Four Seasons Resort, Jimbaran. A simple terracotta pot spills water into a square catchment pond stuffed with irises. Falling water is a good "welcoming" element in any tropical garden.

Hong Kong architects Palmer and Turner designed the benchmark Bali Hyatt lobby to survey the ocean and the central swimming pool. The nearby water gardens, ingeniously designed by Jim Kinoshita of the USA, wrapped around the central facilities. In 1980, Ketut Marsa and I moved in the first Swastika Kebun commando squad to add "ordered jungle" to the impressive landscape architecture. Nineteen years later many of the original gardeners are still tending these gorgeous acres.

Daku, the matriarch of Villa Bebek mongrels, loves a sip of pond water after her morning toast and Vegemite. Good garden design should provide refuge for all flora and fauna.

BALINESE WATER GARDENS

ABOVE: The Balinese "surround" to the water garden at the entrance to the Ganesha Art Gallery was inspired by walls of Bali's coastal temples.

BELOW: Our theme-dream design (a Balinese-Laotian palace) for a noodle cafe at the Four Seasons Resort, Jimbaran Bay, 1998.

Bodies of water are an essential part of a "Balinese Garden" — either as tanks, lotus ponds or even just vats on pedestals filled with dwarf water lilies. The building of large formal water gardens with extensive statuary was once the exclusive domain of rajas and high priests, but today most Balinese homes enjoy the soothing and cooling properties of a picturesque water feature.

A rustic Balinese water garden, with grassy edges and bulrushes, might feature a bamboo pavilion with a thatched roof. A more elaborate version might feature an island, on which could be found an ornamental tree, like a Plumeria or a *Pisonia alba*, a spout or two on a masoned-stone pond edge or a "lantern" nearby to illuminate the scene (yellow and white plants reflect well in the water).

In my work, I like to add stepping stones in Balinese-style ponds. This extra element of "passage" heightens the romantic ambience of a water garden corner. I also like to add walls behind a pond — preferably dripping ferns and orchids.

At the Four Seasons, Jimbaran, I "filled" a tight walled court with a big pond — "using a big idea for a small area" — and made the water garden the "main event". My favourite pond edge materials for Balinese water gardens are brick, grey stone or red laterite as they blend well with grass, green plants and water.

Weeping plants used near the water's edge — Fishtail Ferns, russelia (in a drier climate), spathyglottus, Cane Palms (*Chrysalidocarpus lutescens*) and the Philodendron family — help to "soften" the pond edge and make it look more natural. They are great as "edge-softeners". The weeping willow at a river's edge is the ultimate soft touch landscape accent.

Mossy statues are staples of Balinese water gardens. A large vessel, like a wide-mouthed pot (sealed inside with cement or fibreglass for strength), or a metal vat, makes an interesting miniature Balinese water garden. Placed in the right spot in a courtyard garden, this "moveable feast" can become a striking statement.

BELOW, LEFT: My first garden in Bali, House "C", Batujimbar. Architect: Geoffrey Bawa.

BELOW, RIGHT: Pink lotus, white water lilies and any robust water plant look fine in a fecund Balinese setting. Try to balance the "massing" of water plants with the plants or spaces around the chosen pond.

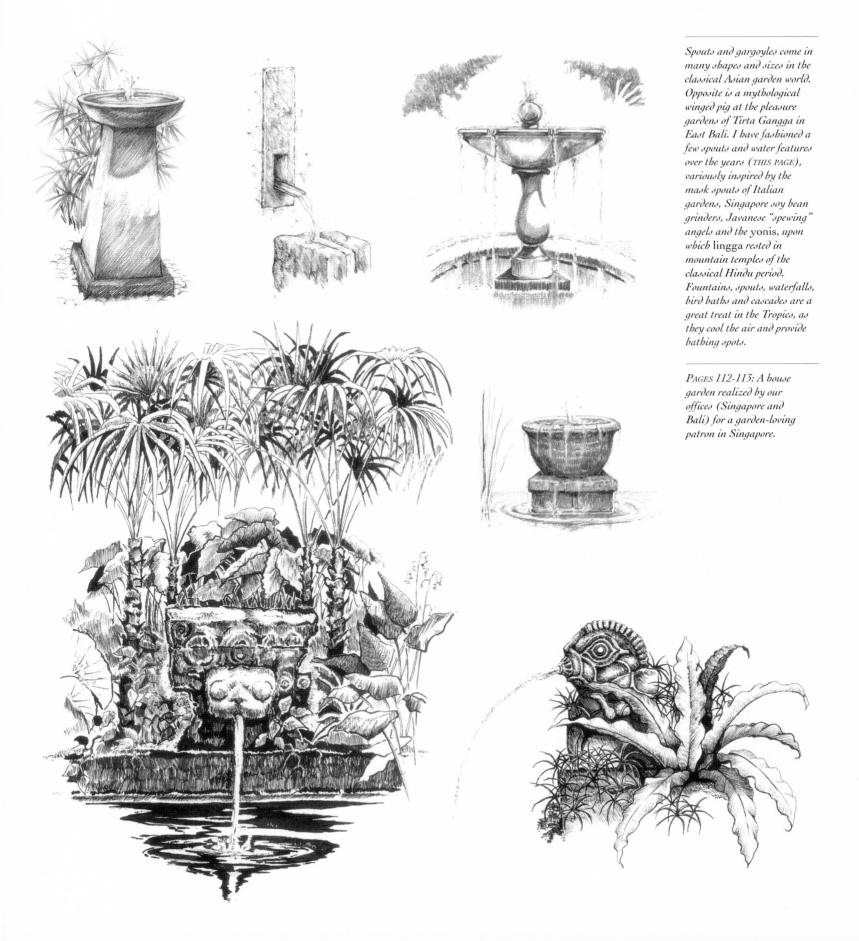

Spouts and gargoyles come in many shapes and sizes in the classical Asian garden world. Opposite is a mythological winged pig at the pleasure gardens of Tirta Gangga in East Bali. I have fashioned a few spouts and water features over the years (THIS PAGE), variously inspired by the mask spouts of Italian gardens, Singapore soy bean grinders, Javanese "spewing" angels and the yonis, upon which lingga rested in mountain temples of the classical Hindu period. Fountains, spouts, waterfalls, bird baths and cascades are a great treat in the Tropics, as they cool the air and provide bathing spots.

PAGES 112-113: A house garden realized by our offices (Singapore and Bali) for a garden-loving patron in Singapore.

Chapter 5

SWIMMING POOLS

"The swimming pool in the Tropics is a symbol of escape and comfort.

How better to clear a head full of humidity than to dive into a cool pool,

float on one's back and watch the surrounding palms silhouetted against a hazy sky?"

he tropical world is the leader in swimming pool design innovation. The availability of relatively cheap and skilled labour puts natural-stone finishes and fancy accents within the budget of most dream home makers and hotel developers. The explosion of tourism in the 1970s and 80s saw the mass-morphing of kidney shapes and lap pools into infinity-edge jaw-droppers and aquatic entertainment complexes. The pool enthusiast today has a dizzying array of choices: saline or chlorine filtration systems; wet or dry edge; glass mosaic, ceramic tile or natural stone lining; bar pool or nay; Jacuzzi appendage or Jacuzzi rampant; nooky niche or sea cow ledge; ladder or stair; pavilion nestling or pool deck party compatible; Hawaiian style, formal or free form; aqua or black (great for reflecting but heats up quickly) and shallow or deep. The market has been so bullish that every six months or so, a major shift seems to have taken place in the conventional wisdom about bathers' taste. Laymen be warned, crack landscapers can dig deep into your psyche based on choices of pool parameters.

What I believe really matters, individual taste aside, is that the pool blends with its site and surroundings. A pool that makes an interesting water garden when not in use is preferable to an aqua oblong that looks a bit sad when unused, like a drive-in cinema during the day. Jungle pools with feeder waterfalls look contrived in small backyards: better a well thought-out water garden or courtyard pool look. Tropical versions of Roman baths have far more pleasure potential. Swimming pools in their own courtyard, particularly the fun-pool variety in extensive grounds and confined by some hedging or enclosing wall, look less like forgotten toys or park utilities. Try to choose a pool shape that matches your requirements (i.e. lapping, lounging or the reticulating *kavetch*, popular in Bali in August).

In selecting the shape and character of a swimming pool one should also consider the pool deck areas to be used — for relaxing, drying of the towels and entertaining. The next big choice would be the choice of water circulation type: overflow (tension or infinity edge) or dry edge.

If you are lucky enough to be designing the landscape for a site that has a commanding view of the ocean, a river or a lake, then the clever Japanese ploy of "borrowing" the neighbouring landscape (adopting it into your own garden design) can be effectively achieved. Try "bleeding" the view-side edge — assuming, of course, a view-side pool. If you are working with a large garden area and are determined to plonk a pool in the middle, the mirage-like look of the full-perimeter tension edge (overflow) sits quite harmoniously in the landscape. Both of these options will afford wonderful special effects for the bather.

PAGE 114: The Villa Bebek pool, Sanur, Bali.

OPPOSITE: The magnificent Amankila pools concertina down a cliff in East Bali.

PAGE 115, LEFT TO RIGHT: Aquatic wonderwoman Valerie Taylor at the Villa Bebek; Hawaiian poolscape at the Grand Bali Beach Hotel; pavilion-style poolscape, Hotel Nusa Dua Beach, Bali.

ABOVE, TOP TO BOTTOM: The Blue Lagoon Club, East Java (1920); Four Seasons Resort pool; Le Meridien Jakarta pool, after the Taman Sari gardens in Central Java.

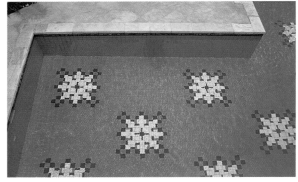

Australian architect Kerry Hill has developed many handsome drainage design solutions in natural stone to replace the unattractive plastic grills, once considered *de rigueur* for the "mirage" pool. The Rasa Sentosa hotel in Singapore, the Sukhothai hotel in Bangkok and the ravishingly simple Serai in Bali have all utilized this special pool edging technique to good effect.

If you and your family and friends like to gorge on hamburgers at the poolside with your ankles in the water, if your pool deck area is restrictively small, or if you would just like a classic architectural pool like the emperor Tiberius, architect Peter Muller and many others before you, then choose the standard skimmers or a continuous drain filtering system and a nice bullnose natural stone pool edge. Big pools in coastal areas can effect a "beach edge" and look most inviting. With the right small-grained sand and a bit of ingenuity you can wade gently into your pool on a simulated sandy foreshore.

The next big decision when designing swimming pools is the colour and type of tile. In the Tropics, dark pools have proven unpopular because they retain heat, and, for the faint-hearted, may harbour "beasties". Bright aqua water, the result when using the common white ceramic tile, is very refreshing but often incongruous in today's spacious and stylish tropical homes. Bluey-greys and bluey-greens, either glass mosaic or ceramic, are a good compromise and match the backdrop of tropical greenery and the limestone or granite hues most often employed in pool deck stone work in the Tropics. True aesthetes use a slate or other natural stone "fascia" between the water line and the pool coping, so that nothing kitchen-like protrudes into the naturally-pristine environment.

TOP: The rustic footbath at the lower swimming pool of the Four Seasons Resort, Bali.

RIGHT: The pond to pool cascade at David Bowie's house in Mustique, St. Vincent and the Grenadines.

ABOVE: Tirta, a batik pattern, on a pool floor in Jakarta. (Tirta means "water" in Javanese.)

ABOVE: Formal Bali-style pool and pavilion in a Singapore house.

LEFT: The Presidential Villa pool at the Four Seasons Resort, Jimbaran, Bali.

CREATING A JUNGLE POOL

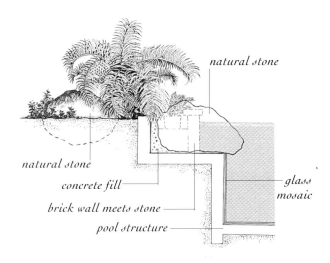

natural stone

natural stone

concrete fill

brick wall meets stone

pool structure

glass mosaic

The hardest thing about making a semi-natural, free-form pool is placing the rocks and waterfall so they look natural. Simulated rocks may not always look fake, but they always feel fake and should be avoided.

The left sketch shows how real boulders should be placed into a pool shell. This is a trick I learned from Jim Nicholay, formerly of Belt Collins International, Singapore, the grandfathers of solid tropical landscape design. Place the rocks so that they will look as natural as possible when partly submerged. Avoid having rock bottoms protruding above the water line like gaping mouths. When submerged the rock should exhibit a smooth lower "edge", with no "lips" protruding above the water line (an old Esther Williams' adage). Brick the rock into its "seat" following the line of the pool shell. Endeavour to leave space on the pool deck to plant rock-hugging plants — *Philodendron sellum, Livistonia chinensis*, Russelia, Pandanus

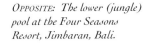

and fishtail ferns all do the job — to "smudge the fudge", as it were. It is important to place rocks in groupings so that they look like a natural outcrop and not like a necklace of giant rabbit droppings around the pool.

Use only natural stone decking, fascias and coping near to the rocks and keep everything a bit rough and untouched, in order to blend. Should you want to create a jungle hillock, in order to be able to install a fake feeder waterfall or "spring", then ensure that there is enough room to "taper back" into the surrounding landscape so that the effect is not silly-hilly.

Place tree ferns, *Phoeonix roebelenii* and *Cycas circinalis* to lean over the rocks and the waterfall for a more tropical jungle look. A cascade pool like this is a real artwork if fashioned sensitively and artistically. Remember: the hardscape must be spot on; the stone chosen should blend with the setting.

OPPOSITE: The lower (jungle) pool at the Four Seasons Resort, Jimbaran, Bali.

BELOW, LEFT: A simple pool with natural stone trim and tiles, set in a bamboo forest at the Taman Bebek hotel, Sayan, Bali — the use of natural stone (or clever fake stone) is a must when creating a jungle pool.

BELOW, RIGHT: The incredible rock pool at the Four Seasons Ka'upulehu, Hawaii.

POOL FURNITURE

RIGHT: A rustic towel rack, made of drift wood, and a lavastone soap dish at the beachside hot spa dip pool adjacent to the cool water rock pool of the Four Seasons Resort at Ka'upulehu, Hawaii.

BELOW: Rows of chaises-longues hover, mirage-like, at the pool of the Bali Inter-Continental Resort, Jimbaran .

Americans seem to have the best tradition of pool furniture, perhaps because they were collectively raised on a diet of Californian glamour where starlets and movie stars "lounging poolside" were part of the Hollywood myth. Solid black metal *chaises-longues* with yellow and white striped, or cadmium blue, upholstery, established a tradition. Tropical hardwood furniture — with khaki covers — strong, sleek and simple are elegant and unobtrusive. (Ed Tuttle's designs for the Sukhothai in Bangkok were the best of their generation.)

Horrid white plastic pool furniture is to be shunned at all cost. My other pet hates are chunky, carved, arts-and-crafts versions that are as suitable parked poolside as a Bavarian chest. Pergolas adjacent to pools are a must, especially useful in an era when people want to avoid the sun's harmful rays. A shady tree is another blessing — especially for the collagen-challenged seeking respite.

Thai *sala* pavilions with their platform beds (*futon* optional) and triangular relax cushions are a glamorous alternative to *chaises-longues* and umbrellas.

LEFT: *At the Villa Bebek pool Chippendale-inspired lounge chairs and an antique occasional table define a breakfast nook.*

BELOW: *Day-beds with Thai-style end cushions create an open-air belvedere space at a Filipino beach-side pool.*

SPAS, HEALTH AND SPORTS CLUBS

Spas are the new growth area of landscape design. As hotels and resorts "beef up" their facilities, designers are being called upon to design atmospheric settings for hot and cold plunge pools, private massage courtyards and relaxation terraces. It is an invigorating design area, to say the least, as it calls on a designer's experience in swimming-pool design (the decks, pool furniture and fun aspects), walled-court-yard design (a product of the massage room's privacy requirements) and a sense of the romantic that people want in their sports, relaxation and treatment areas.

Traditionally the *therma* of Italy, the spas of Germany, the crater lake-side hot springs of Java and Bali and the *hammam* of the Arab world provide stylish and luxurious antecedents for the "new" tropical spa design. Many new eco-tourism developments in the tropical world — Coeren Cove on South Stradbroke Island in Queensland, Australia; the Shangri-La Spa in Naples, Florida; the Four Seasons Resort Spa in Hawaii; and village-like complexes in Thailand and Indonesia, to name but a few of the hundreds that opened in the 1990s — feature state-of-the-art lap pools and attractive gardens that are a big part of their drawing power.

For garden designers it is a specialist area, and a challenging one — any tropical garden world tour should take in some of these wonders.

TOP: The original Southeast Asian spas were royal baths sculpted around natural springs. Water gushed from stomach cakras of fertility goddesses. The springs had special enclosures (seen here in the centre) for the gathering of water to be used in the manufacture of tirta amerta, the elixir of life. Some springs had healing properties, others were fountains of youth.

ABOVE : My office designed this Majapahit-style spout-fountain wall for a pool in a private house in Jakarta.

PAGES 124–25: A jungle pool I worked on with Bill Bensley at Wantilan Lama, Batujimbar, Sanur. Monstera deliciosa, cane palms, Plumerias and oleanders crowd in on this secluded natural-stone pool.

RIGHT: A plan of the men's hot and cold dip pools at the Four Seasons Resort spa, Jimbaran, Bali. It is an idyllic courtyard retreat in the tradition of colonial sports clubs, with their space and piles of fluffy towels. I used a palette of "modernist" plants in terracotta pots — (a) Pandanus, (b) Cordyline indivisa, (c) White Pampas Grass, (d) Boston fern, (e) Raphis excelsa (f) purple ground orchids (Spathoglotis plicata).

OPPOSITE: A jungle spa in the beautiful mountain resort Begawan Giri in Bali.

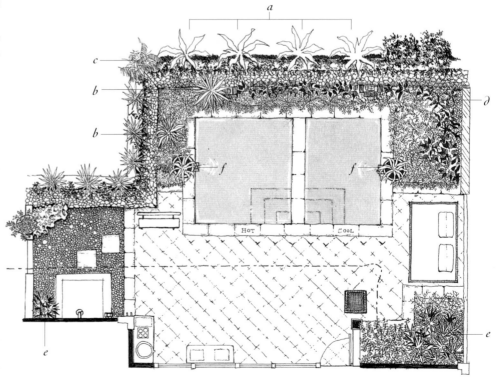

Chapter 6

PLANTING SCHEMES

" ... though 'copying' nature is impossible, by observation its 'motives' can be translated into garden spaces in aesthetic terms."

PENELOPE HOBHOUSE, *NATURAL PLANTING*

The variety of plants in the Tropics is staggering — there are 15,000 varieties of palms alone. Every day, a new strain of Heliconia (flowering banana) is born in the jungles of South America and a new medicinal use found for some rainforest regular. But these are matters of botany and horticulture. As a garden designer you need to aquaint yourself with the families of tropical shrubs, trees, palms and water plants in order to compose planting schemes.

A garden designer is part sculptor, part engineer and part mid-wife, for his "paint box" is filled with living things. Horticulture is the science of gardens; landscape design the art of utilizing nature — as inspiration, muse and hand-maiden.

For the first stage in garden design, one needs to use one's heart, to feel the spirit of the land, and get what the Japanese call a "point of view". Then one needs to use one's head, to imagine how the shaping of nature can be achieved. Experience is then drawn upon to run though the mind's "data bank" of plant information and cross reference it with site suitability, and with given elements — the architecture and the user's taste. Taste then can be employed to give the work flavours. If you have an artistic or poetic eye (it's a bit like a musical ear) you can embellish your work with your own "line", in the choice of plant combinations, artworks and hardscape elements.

Paths, pond edges, boundary walls and pergolas are, in a sense, the frames or easels for one's garden painting; but they should also form an integral part of the visual composition, and need to be carefully thought out and designed. Garden design is not about "filling in between the static bits" but about creating studies or compositions of nature, be they artful or municipal.

Great garden design involves knowledge, *and* all the senses, *and* the passion of the restless soul of the artist. In this chapter I will delve into the character of tropical plants and trees and their effect on a composition. I have chosen to use artists' works to illustrate my ideas, as I find that a gardener's hand is best understood by an artist's eye. Cameras rarely catch the hidden meanings.

Plants and trees have characters — some are loving, others destructive; some are shy, some "present like a baboon" — and they also have physical attributes, such as their texture, shape, line and colour. Horticulturists study plants one by one. A landscaper must know the plants and all their above-mentioned attributes, and must have the talent to create combinations — like composing symphonies — which are imaginative. "What's the problem?" I sometimes whinge to clients uneducated in the symphonic possibilities of garden art, "Too many leaves?"

There are "movements" in a large garden, to continue the analogy, with "theme" plants and brass sections. Colour, of course, plays a huge part in garden design,

ABOVE, TOP TO BOTTOM:
Areca Palms surround
a Pagan temple; a large
Plumeria obtusa in
the grounds of a
Sri Lankan hotel designed
by Geoffrey Bawa;
topiary Bambis in a
Saigon villa garden.

PAGE 130: The fabulous
Zobel Estate gardens
in Calatagan,
the Philippines.

PAGE 131, LEFT TO RIGHT:
Dracaena marginata
in a compact corner; a
19th-century horticultural
print; a courtyard planting
in Thailand; English-style
tropical planting.

PAGES 132–133: The palm
section of the Hilton hotel
garden in Bangkok.

OPPOSITE: The Aloe,
Cactus and Yucca valley
of the Four Seasons Resort,
Jimbaran, Bali.

ABOVE, TOP TO BOTTOM:
Sakiko Ibuchi's painting of
the Bali Hyatt parklands,
Sanur; Pritchardia palms in
the grounds of an Hawaiian
hotel; a Bird's-nest Fern in
a Singapore garden.

particularly in tropical gardens, where coloured leaves and the interplay of leaf and trunk shapes are often called upon to provide the variety that spring brings gardens in temperate climes. The wet season is a time, for example, when many of the tropical world's colour plants — the bougainvilleas and hibiscuses in particular — go into green "growing" cycles. All the "lime green" colours, of fresh leaves and moss, take over the composition. For this reason, the artful combination of textures and shapes — fan-like palm fronds mixed with spiky cordylines and soft dewy ground covers, for example — is of prime importance in a tropical garden. The French painter Rousseau's dreamscapes of violent Heliconias rampant were a bit far-fetched, but a well-planned tropical garden can induce a sense of outrage. Even the names of many popular tropical plants — Red Hot Poker, Devil's Trumpet, African Tulip — evince a sense of boldness and theatre.

The choice of the right trees is another steep learning curve in tropical garden design: choose the wrong species and it could bring your house down in a matter of months! There are great spreading trees whose canopies encompass the area of a football field, and erect trees whose "above the ground" root systems stop Jeeps in their tracks. Some flowering trees, like the September Tree and the Tabubuaya, swamp the ground knee-deep in petals. Others display giant "corsages" of blooms above their crown, like the African Tulip and the Bauhinia — which are good viewed from first-floor verandahs. Other trees droop flowers, like the *Cassia fistula* "Golden Rain Tree" and the *Erythrina crista-galli*, and some even dangle "sausages"! The Cannonball Tree explodes in your face with an immaculate orange and coral pink bloom, shoulder high, on the majestic tree's trunk.

The tropical world is particularly rich in small flowering trees like the Plumerias, the oleander, the Caesalpinia (peacock plants) and the *Jatropha pandiflora*, all of which flower almost all year round. The seeds of many palms — like the MacArthur Palm (*Ptychosperma macarthurii*) and the Fishtail Palm (*Caryota mitis*) and all the palms called Alexandra and Manila — have beautiful seed displays, like giant drop earrings, in all the colours of the rainbow. Even the Coconut Palms come in giant, green, yellow and dwarf, with coconuts to match; not to mention the thousands of varieties of bananas, which

provide almost instant 'fill' to tropical parkland settings — their gently swaying leaves catching the sunlight like butterflies' wings.

Plum Rhoeo and silver pot-pourri ground covers, white waving costus and the almost spherical Crinum family, in all its colours, are just a few of the many "artistic" plant elements in the ground cover and flowering shrub range, that can be added to give "spice" to a tropical landscape composition.

Choosing a "theme plant" that nestles well in the neighbourhood or belongs in that environment — like pandanus on the coast or ferns in the mountains — is an excellent starting point. Plants are just the notes on a floral symphony. It is composition and balance that make the melody stick.

Hopefully, this chapter will inspire you to be rather brave with your tropical garden compositions, whilst also respecting the unique and unusual way that one can employ even the most pedestrian of plants.

For the large courtyard gardens of the Bali Hyatt Sanur, I worked with Ketut Marsa of Swastika Kebun to create rich colourful areas that were inspired, in part, by the bursts of colour and movement one finds in coral gardens under the sea. The palette of plants is simple, even pedestrian, but the result is quite dramatic.

SHAPES IN NATURE

A lone Phoenix palm on the Adyar river in front of the Madras Club in Channai, South India.

BELOW: Tropical trees, like the Royal Poinciana (Delonix regia), flower more than twice a year if in a sandy soil.

Sculpting miniature landscapes or realizing nature in miniature is an essential skill for a good garden designer. So too is knowing how to make a natural-ist design look effortless and yet artful. Effortless, because Mother Nature is the best garden designer (and She doesn't try too hard); artful, because our sense of beauty, nay our sense of appreciation of beautiful gardens, is often triggered by natural cues such as horizons, reflections, interesting silhouettes and attractive sequences of volumes rather like the grand canyon. The shaping of "volumes" of plant material is the basis of good garden design: the flowers, artworks, water bod-ies and other features are but the accessories.

I like to think of a garden as a set on a theatre stage. One has a backdrop, (the garden's boundary wall, a forest or a skyline), and a proscenium arch (the verandah's eave, a window frame, or the garden entrance gate). Then there are various "flats", i.e. banks of planted areas or borders. Some of the "volumes" are

human height, soft and round (like the panitera, the Acalypha and the hibisci), whilst others are knee high and spiky (such as the Rhoeo, crotons and agaves). In the corner of the set are wee washes of ground-cover, and centre stage the odd stately trunk which divides up space and adds sculptural interest. It is important that the ordering of these "volumes" looks natural as they head for the edge of the composition. Small trees and palm clumps help one taper back a planting scheme. Try oleanders, cane palms, MacArthur (or Hurricane) Palms, Plumeria and Pampas Grass to achieve a natural look and a balanced composition. The stage should also be properly lit, if the garden is to be enjoyed at night (see chapter 8).

In tropical gardening one has to consider that extra dimension of rapid growth. The landscape designer must be aware of the potential for quite radical change to the balance of shapes during a garden's adolescence (which lasts for the first 12 months!). It is almost like designing a not-too-slow motion kinetic artwork. Some of my European friends and hotel guests I have met in Bali seem to abhor the gusto with which tropical gardeners attack foliage during the wet season. However, when shaping a garden in the Tropics, you have to be harsh in order to maintain healthy growth and a balanced, not messy composition. Wilderness gardens are not a sensible option in the Tropics — wild grasses harbour wild beasts. By all means let your tropical garden run amok but be prepared for the invasion of fungi, bugs and possibly snakes that thrive in tropical bush. A good tropical garden needs plenty of sun and air, the former to soak up the moisture after heavy rains and the latter to blow away the bugs.

During peak periods in the wet season, a mature tropical garden can be "thinned out", exposing all the brand-new palm fronds and healthy branches. This gives the garden a spruced-up, almost polished look, and allows more air and light to enter and circulate in the moisture-laden mass. In tropical pruning you should be bold. Carve out big curves and elliptical "windows" in the planting scheme to open vistas and frame patches of sky. At the height of the wet season, when the ficus have started growing in the gutters, creepers should be ripped off statues, walls and tree trunks, and ground-covers cut right back. Wade in with a machete before the pergolas turn to a pulpy mush. This sort of "radical pruning" is part and parcel of the nature shaping cycle of a mature tropical garden.

Design a garden with pockets of both and you will be rewarded with sensual shadows and wafts of fresh fragrance. Drape, chip, preen and prune — these skills are all part of the sculptor's art. Think about the framework of the garden first, then add the sparklers. Soften with impurity.

Roll out a picnic mat. Enjoy!

TOP: Geoffrey Bawa's incredible English-Italianate tropical garden, Lunuganga, in Sri Lanka features many "sublime moments" — not the least of which is this lake view seen from the main house terrace, framed by an arching Plumeria obtusa *branch with a sensual Perseus statue "under its wing".*

ABOVE: A courtyard in the Villa Bebek with a Bougainvillea stem snaking up a Plumeria "host".

THE SOFTENING TOUCH

The entrance porch to a family mansion in Georgetown, Penang, Malaysia is "softened" by the caressing fronds of Areca triandra *and* Pinanga adangensis.

Most architecture is improved by the addition of garden elements — that one Date Palm in front of the pyramids at Giza, for example, makes all the difference. Plants soften edges and frame views: the right ground cover "washing" over a curb or retaining bank will make a daunting set of steps look like a stairway to heaven. Pergolas with gently weeping vines soften building façades, and make shady nooks from which to admire views that have been framed by tentacles of foliage.

Small-leafed "fancies" in the form of maidenhair ferns or small-leafed ground covers can be added to the corners of tropical gardens — that is, in the cracks of paving or on the skirting of a courtyard wall. This will create a more romantic composition, after the spirit of the pre-Raphaelite painters.

Gentle creepers can be trained across wall tops and fine orchids added to tree trunks to achieve the same softening effect. In the Tropics the *Ficus pumila* — the rather moss-like creeping fig — can turn a hard boundary wall or stone embankment into a topiary hedge in a matter of months. Creepers like Scindapsus or epiphytes like Bird's-nest Ferns can also be added to walls and tree trunks to provide a glossy coat of thick shapely leaves.

Most tropical "softeners" of this nature need to be regularly trimmed back as it is the nascent "teenage" growth that looks prettiest. Many of these "creepy-crawlies" can grow to giant proportions if allowed to mature, with the potential to clog up a view or cause damage to a masoned wall. Reticence is the keynote here.

In some Hawaiian gardens, Bromeliads and Spanish Moss are added to soften stark tree trunks, and baby antheriums planted at the ankles of Alexandra Palm (*Archontophoenix alexandrae*) clumps — all in the name of "softening".

Borders can be softened by the addition of ground covers at their outer edge — in this instance with an ornamental dwarf Lantana. In the background Pisonia alba *leaves and curly-tailed yellow codiaeums soften the hedge of acalaphi and hibisci.*

The labyrinthine planter-box passages around the central facilities and guest wings of the Bali Hyatt in Sanur required a lot of softening: we used the "Lee Kwan Yew Vine" (Hoya sikkimensis), Wedelia trilobata, dwarf Lantana creepers and Bougainvillea spectabilis (the purple small leaf variety) to "smudge" the hard edges.

The stairs in the foreshore parklands of the Four Seasons Resort in Jimbaran, Bali, were designed to "nestle" into soft clouds of russelia (with its tails of red-belled foliage), Pseuderanthemum atropurpureum (whose smart crimson and violet flowers poke daintily above the foliage crown), and the gentle Hibiscus rosa sinensis (whose small green leaves, vibrant red flowers and "loose" shape work well with the two aforementioned plants).

COLOUR AND MOVEMENT

ABOVE: The bold streaked red leaves of the Cordyline terminalis, *captured by artist Sakiko Ibuchi in the Bali Hyatt Sanur gardens.*

RIGHT: Lilac-flowered Bromeliads in a bed of baby rhoeos in Dennis Hundscheidt's garden, Brisbane, Queensland.

OPPOSITE, TOP: Banks of Heliconia and crotons (Codiaeum) provide bursts of colour in this Filipino garden. A good serving of coloured perennials is a common design ploy in large tropical gardens.

OPPOSITE, BELOW: The colourful opaque leaves of the Heliconia and Cordyline family.

I have long been fascinated by Mother Nature's design models for humans — redheads, brunettes, albinos and blacks, to name a few — and the way in which her designs are repeated in the worlds of flora and fauna. There are *alba* (blonde), *purpurea* (brunette) and *tricolora* (ruddy) versions of most ornamental plants as well as hairy, spiky, shiny and dull versions within the sub-species. Each plant has its own character and its own strengths and weaknesses. Some look good en masse, like most palms; others look best solitary, like many ornamental courtyard plants.

When designing a planting scheme in a garden one needs to think about the plants' characteristics: the growing patterns; their overall shape at maturity; their effect en masse, and their effect when mixed with other plants; the way they flower; the way they behave in the wet season (do they lose all colour in their leaves, for example, or stop flowering due to lack of sun like the bougainvillea); and the combinations of leaf colours and shapes. All this must be taken into account, in addition to imagining the effect the planned "plant massing" has on the architecture, the surroundings, one's heart strings and one's purse strings. One has to juggle a lot of balls in garden design.

Certain colours in nature do not go together — yellows and lilacs, for example — and certain groupings of coloured-leaved plants can be overly "polychromatic", if a more subtle naturalism is desired. In larger gardens, mass plantings of coloured plants and ground-covers alleviates the overbearing greenness that comes with a tropical garden in the wet season. Theme gardens based on flower colours are popular in temperate climate gardens but rarely experimented with in tropical gardens. Think of the following pages as this book's tropical "colour section".

MELLOW YELLOW

Sakiko Ibuchi's drawing of a solitary Washingtonia palm in the noon sun in the palm section of the Bali Hyatt Horticultural Garden.

The golden yellow flower of the Lobster-claw Heliconia is a solid performer — thrusting up flowers with a relatively long "shelf life". The flowers can easily be gathered by pulling hard on their stems. They make striking flower arrangements when used en masse.

The yellow Pandanus is a very sturdy plant that stays bright canary yellow through-out the year. It can grow into a multi-branched tree over five years — its tentacle-like support roots piercing down from the tree's branches into the ground which helps with the stability of this floppy leafed wonder's stability.

The botanical category *alba* refers to the albino variants of plants, sometimes variegated with a white tinge or streak, sometimes totally white (like Pampas Grass, *Arundinaria variegata*). "Alba" is also used for most plants with a yellow-variegated look, of which there are many in the Tropics. The screaming canary-yellow Pisonia (see photo below) is at one end of the range and the moody daffodil-yellow water lilies, with their khaki and bronze-green leaves, at the other.

The "money plant", the streaked yellow and green Scindapsus, is one plant found in nearly all tropical gardens, as is the broad leafed *Heliconia robusta alba* which comes in many different yellow and green combinations. Yellow bamboo is another yellow-streaked-with-green favourite of garden planners. In the Gading Garden I created at the Bali Hyatt Sanur (*gading* being the Indonesian word for this yellow-green colour freak of nature), I used terracotta bricks as pavers and various terracotta pots as accent artworks to create an unusual colour scheme that is uniquely tropical. This garden is next to the tropical "White Garden" I created to honour Vita Sackville-West's famous white garden at Sissinghurst Castle in Kent, England. I used a palette of Pandanus, Heliconia, Pleomele, Scindapsus, Duranta and yellow water lilies to recreate the desired mellow yellow look (see photo page 50). Many variegated varieties of popular plants — Hibiscus, Codiaeum (crotons), and the Pandanus in particular, get brighter or more shriekingly yellow at their tips due to the extra exposure to the sun.

This creates an effect not unlike that in snowcapped winter gardens where extremities are tinged with extra definition. The same effect can be used in tropical compositions to achieve more dramatic impact or resolution.

ABOVE: An arbour of the subtropical Laburnum vossii *in Bodnant Garden, Wales, UK.*

LEFT: A mature Pisonia alba *tree provides a splash of yellow in a thickly planted area of the Bali Hyatt in Sanur.*

TROPICAL WHITE GARDENS

Sakiko Ibuchi's crayon drawing of the Bali Hyatt Sanur "White Garden After Vita" by night. White plants are particularly effective in catching any stray moonbeams.

OPPOSITE, TOP: A glade of Spider Lilies (Hymenocallis littoralis) *and white plumeria create a fresh "snow-tipped" look.*

OPPOSITE, BOTTOM, LEFT TO RIGHT: White Pampas Grass (Cortaderia selloana), *variegated crinum, and white* Thunbergia grandiflora *provide strong streaks of white throughout the wet season.*

RIGHT: A cluster of white-tipped Bromeliads catches the eye amidst the verdant splendour of Dennis Hundscheidt's Brisbane garden.

Having visited Vita Sackville-West's famous white garden at Sissinghurst, in Kent in 1979, I returned to the Tropics to try my hand at a fresh theme court of tropical white plants in a small patch at the Bali Hyatt Sanur's extensive Horticultural Garden. It became a small outdoor "ante-chamber" replete with obelisks, carpet planting and a central fountain with a pond featuring albino salamanders.

I discovered alba varieties of plants I never knew existed and learnt to love the freshness and the blooms a strand of climbing white jasmine or tumbling night-blooming cestrum brings to an otherwise boringly verdant garden. I learned how cooling white and green are together, especially near terracotta pavers or Roman brick walls, and how tender are the white flowered varieties of old friends — such as the Hibiscus, Bougainvillea, oleander and Gardenia. Certain tropical high-performers — like the white *Thunbergia grandiflora*, Plumeria family, and Mussaenda — are exceptions to this rule. On the other hand, white variegated leaf plants — such as the Agaves, various white grasses and bamboos — thrive even in sub-tropical climate zones. Bushy white-leafed plants can be employed to dramatic effect in a garden composition. They can be used to create a white starburst or a splash of brightness; or used to provide the scenic "flats" which help make interesting edges.

White attracts the eye. Something white, or bright yellow for that matter, at the end of a long vista or a small garden will help create a sense of depth. White leaves also take artificial light well, and a garden can take on a whole new look at night with the judicious lighting of its lighter and whiter elements. Unlit white gardens are particularly romantic on moonlit nights.

Chapter 7

PLANTS

"*We journeyed in a land of flowers and ideal tropical vegetation, under smiling skies, along roads shaded by clustering palm trees and made gay with miles upon miles of small arches of ribbon-like fringes of tender leaves.*"

HENRY STEEL OLCOTT, *OLD DIARY LEAVES*

o create gardens, one must love nature and understand plants. God *is* the best gardener; we are here but to emulate. To start, one has to observe the patterns of nature: the leaf patterns, the growing patterns, the patterns of climate and the lay of the land. One must comprehend the different stages of a ground-cover's, shrub's, or tree's life cycle and how it behaves, at each stage, and in differing soil and site conditions. Once you get the garden-loving bug, nature becomes a source of everlasting amazement — so whimsical, eccentric and loveable are her flora.

This chapter will focus on just a few of the characteristics and properties of the main plant families in the tropical world from the point of view of design. It is more useful, I have learnt, to know more about a few plants (like their seasonal behaviour) than a little about a lot of plants. When making one's first choice in selecting plants for a garden scheme, think of the design task for which they may be needed — to grow tall and compact to hide a telegraph pole, for example, or spread a broad canopy for a children's playground — and then "accessorize" with exotics. Observe nature when travelling and learn the growing cycles and growth patterns of your favourites. It is a complex science, the art of gardening, and the harnessing of plants, to make beauty, a most demanding artform.

If a plant looks "old hat" in a neighbourhood, it's probably because it's proven to be a good performer in the local soil and climatic conditions. Choose the plant that's right for the job, not some trendy *arriviste*. A big vocabulary never helped anyone be a better writer. Virtuosity in planting design comes with experience and observation, not just a big budget.

ABOVE: An 18th-century Dutch print of an early plantation in the East Indies

LEFT: Dutch Artist W.O.J. Nieuwenkamp's etching (1910) of the main road in Mataram, Lombok, Indonesia.

OPPOSITE: A rare Ficus throws bizarre shadows in an Hawaiian parkland setting.

PAGE 148 : A perfect canopy — a Leopard Tree in the old Government House grounds adjacent to the Brisbane Botanic Gardens.

PAGE 149, LEFT TO RIGHT: Yellow Bamboo, the pink lotus flower, a botanical drawing of a palm tree, and a pink Plumeria in K.R.T. Hardjonegoro's classic Surakartan garden.

PAGE 150–51: The yellow (variegated) garden adjacent to "The White Garden" at the Bali Hyatt Sanur.

TREES AS CANOPIES

ABOVE: Two mighty Banyan trees drawn by Dutch artist W.O.J. Nieuwenkamp in 1912.

BELOW: A popular outdoor "reading room" in the Brisbane Botanic Garden.

OPPOSITE: A grove of coastal trees, called camplung *trees, in Balinese, in the foreshore parklands of the Bali Hyatt, Sanur.*

Certain umbrella-like trees and shrubs provide huge pools of shade, for respite from the blazing sun, and a spot to sit quietly and read a book. Most traditional villages around the equator have at their centre platforms of rock (see Compang, page 188) or grassy knolls under a giant shade tree.

Because of the shelter they offer, these areas often become used as bus stops, goat markets and offering platforms (to the spirit of the tree, after the lesson of the Gautama Buddha under his Bodhi Tree, *Ficus religiosa*).

Good tropical garden designers use canopy trees extensively, especially near car parks, and at various intervals throughout the garden, to provide puddles of deep dark shade and refuge. The smaller canopy trees can also be used as a frame: the appreciation of the garden is enhanced by viewing it through tortured limbs. A thoughtfully arranged group of canopy trees creates a maze of sinewy shapes (see photo right) as does a row of palms a "chorus line".

FERNS

A Stag-horn Fern in a coastal garden in Kuta, Bali.

OPPOSITE, CLOCKWISE FROM TOP LEFT: the Fishtail Fern (Nephrolepsis exaltata bostonensis), tree ferns and crawling ferns (Humata tyermanii) are great "softeners" in any garden; many ferns attach themselves readily to statues and cracks in courtyard walls; ferns take the morning light beautifully, and glisten after a rainstorm.

Ferns are the fungus-world's star performers: they can appear, like adolescent down, on a window ledge or sprout like sea urchins in the fork of a majestic rain tree. Rarely invasive, the moisture-loving epiphytes (ferns that attach to a host but don't "sap its energy") are the drop-earrings and handle-bar moustaches (see photos left and below) of the plant world. Ground ferns and brackens are excellent "softeners" — they "smudge" the hard lines of garden artworks. They are also excellent ground covers (as are Bird's-nest Ferns) in full-blooded "tropicana" compositions, as a shaggy carpet-like base for mixtures of palms and heliconias and cordylines.

Ferns are easy to grow, easy to transplant (provided there's lots of moisture), and easier still to propagate (from "sporom" tufts of the root). Many of the crawling or creeping varieties do need cutting back or thinning out, regularly, to avoid the "compacted bristle look". Fern growth can be encouraged on porous surfaces by the regular use of fertilizer and water.

Bird's-nests Ferns and Maidenhair Ferns look particularly impressive on verandah pedestals, and in planter pots they become positively ballerina-like (see photograph below). Tree ferns, on the other hand, are difficult to maintain in all but the most humid conditions — spaghetti-like irrigation pipes must drip water into their crowns during the dry season.

Unfurling wispy zippers of verdant delight, the Fishtail Ferns (opposite top left) are great performers in nearly all tropical micro-climates and soil types: ferns are the feathers of tropical garden design.

RIGHT: Bird's-nest Ferns are great "fill" material in fully equatorial climates. They thrown out "arms" in an eternal gesture of embracing the sun.

GROUND COVERS

TOP AND ABOVE: The humble Hemigraphis is a hardy plum and silver-coloured ground cover that is very easy to propagate. It grows well in dappled light and in a shallow top soil.

OPPOSITE, BOTTOM: The Bromeliads and "wandering Jew" ground-cover in Dennis Hundscheidt's Brisbane garden.

OPPOSITE, TOP: The terraces of the Bali Hyatt, Sanur, were originally planted with grass, and with a border of "Lee Kuan Yew Vine" (Hoya sikkimensis). In 1984, I redesigned the hotel's softscape and added mass — plantings of colourful white Alternanthera bettzickiana aurea, red Iresine herbstii acuminata and yellow Wedelia trilobata ground-covers. The mass plantings, based, loosely, on Matisse cut-outs were then sprinkled with "accent clumps" of Alpinia purpurata and white cacti.

Grass is the most practical of ground covers — its thick "pelt" is clean and maintenance-friendly. It is versatile and an ideal surface for sunning towels, running toddlers, practising golf, and it provides a verdant outdoor carpet as a respite from tropical bushiness. Coconut groves, front lawns and golf courses are three great cultural icons of the garden world.

Small areas of grass forced onto a landscape design, can, however, look marginalized. I always think that the overall composition in a small tropical garden needs to incorporate grass in a meaningful way or not at all. A tiny area of struggling, sodden grass is the garden equivalent of the pastry left over from a cookie cutting exercise! A rustic paving or a shade-loving ground cover is perhaps a better design choice. Make sure when deciding grass that you are choosing the right type — whether Cow Grass, Manila Grass, tufty Japanese Grass, or Couch — for the particular soil and sunlight conditions.

If you should decide to go with a ground cover plant in a courtyard, instead of grass, make sure that you know its growth cycle. The main purpose of ground covers is to hide the soil. Balding and patchy growth is unsightly. Many of the more attractive ground covers — like Coleus, Wedelia, creeping fern and Portulaca — need seasonal replanting or cutting back.

Ground-covers such as Mondograss (Othiopogon), in all its many shapes and various sizes, and the humble Rhoeo are great tropical performers because they are hardy and "fill in" easily around accent plants and other shrubs. They are dark in hue, which provides a good backdrop for the flowers and other sun-seeking "stars" of the tropical garden (such as the new palm fronds, the fresh strands of Pampas Grass and the dripping vines).

In large gardens, one can create great blocks of instant colour (see photo below right) with the clever use of colourful ground covers; for example, white cacti, golden Scindapsus, plum-coloured Rhoeo, smokey silver Bromeliads or glossy lime-green Wedelia. In smaller courtyard spaces one can add mixes of ground covers, creating charming miniature gardens in the corners of the courtyard space, or at the "ankles" of shade trees and shrubs.

With ground covers, choosing the right "bits and pieces", or carpets of colour, is the penultimate touch in a garden's design. It should be executed after the placement of the hardscape elements, the artworks and the lighting, and before the draping of softscape orchids and vines.

Personally, I always try to intersperse a few specimens of the surrounding plant selection into beds of ground covers, as a "forced leaching" if you like, to give a composition a more natural and spontaneous look.

BAMBOO

TOP: *The unique silhouette of the blade-like leaves of Giant Green Bamboo* (Dendrocalamus giganteus).

ABOVE: *Bamboo growing in cracks of a rubble wall in the Penang Arboretum, in Malaysia.*

OPPOSITE: *Different bamboo varieties exhibit different characteristics.* CLOCKWISE, FROM TOP LEFT: *Bambusa vulgaris as a clump of feather-like poles; Buddha's Belly Bamboo* (Bambusa ventricosa) *with its distinctive knobby stems; the cathedral's ceiling effect of equally spaced clumps of Giant Green Bamboo; bamboo growing in a tropical rainforest.*

Bamboo is the landscaper's friend — all manner of pergolas, fences, gates, furniture, steps and even whole houses, including the shingles (see photo page14), can be fashioned from the ever-giving clumps.

Aesthetically, the thousands of varieties of bamboo are the "sequins and beads" of a landscaper's tool box — they add a touch of class to any garden design. Whether as a tsunami-like forest of cascading leaves or as a pristine clump of black beauty in the centre of a Japanese court, bamboo never goes unnoticed. The tropical varieties of bamboo, all members of the grass family, range from the Giant Green found inscribed with love poems in the Quandong Botanic Garden, to the piquant Crawling Dwarf which grows in dewy crevasses across the equator. Few other plants like to grow with bamboo, so vicious are its roots. It is therefore best used on its own, or planted alongside other bamboos. Amongst tropical varieties, the knobbly Buddha's Belly Bamboo (*Bambusa ventricosa*) and the glamorous Golden Yellow are the prima ballerinas of horticultural accents. Other bamboo varieties fulfil less starry roles. "Workhorses" like the Hedge Bamboo (*Pseudososa japonica*), Ostrich Feather and Fish-pole Bamboo (*Phyllostachys aurea*) are very useful when hedging or screening are required along a boundary.

Bamboo poles moan, leaves rustle, like shaken castanets, as the wind passes through. The shadows of bamboo leaves are like painted raindrops.

Bamboos do not grow well in pots, or indoors — they are wild plants that demand respect. Chinese gardeners train tropical bamboo into box shapes and curlicues. Modernists love to use bamboo's unique "look" — the sparrows' legs and feathery foliage — as a counterpoint to hard, glossy architectural finishes. Personally, I love the gothic arch tunnels of bamboo-lined avenues, and the speckled glistening light of bamboo forests after rain.

Many cultures have reverence for the bamboo plant. Hindus believe bamboo should never be planted on a Sunday. The Balinese use knives fashioned from the "semi-divine" yellow bamboo to cut babies from their mothers umbilical chord. The Sasaks of Lombok are named after the bamboo rafts, called *sesek*, that carried them from Java to Lombok some 600 years ago. In Jamaica, rock impresario Chris Blackwell has created a museum of bamboo instruments. In the Philippines, fresh bamboo shoots are cooked and eaten as a delicacy.

Bamboo is far more versatile as a product than as an addition to a planting scheme. It can look interesting united with some vines, or holding its own in a courtyard "duet" with a stand of palms. But its real decorative charm is as a stand or clump of poles, poking nobly out of a garden floor. Any bamboo is fiercely deciduous: make sure your sweeping arm is up to it before using lots of the leggy wonder.

VINES AND CREEPERS

The Scindapsus vine. or Money Plant, comes in many varieties. The variegated Epipremnum pinnarum "aureum" (formerly known as Scindapsus aureus) is a robust climber that can cover the trunks of a palm grove in a matter of months (see photo of Bali Hyatt, Sanur, page 19).

OPPOSITE, CLOCKWISE FROM TOP LEFT: Bougainvillea on a pergola-covered bridge; an arch of Bougainvillea spectabilis mixed with Antigonon leptopus over the entrance gates to the Institut Teknologi Bandung in West Java, Indonesia; the tenacious Thunbergia grandiflora vine in a Plumeria host tree.

BELOW: A corner of Villa Made at the Taman Bebek Hotel in Sayan, Bali. A "corsage" of Monstera floats above the indoor-outdoor living area.

BELOW, RIGHT: The living fences of the Four Seasons Resort, Jimbaran, are not vines as commonly thought but the branches of fertile Santen trimmed into balustrade-like vine barriers.

The tropical world, with its moist air and often rich volcanic soil, has an abundance of tentacle-like vines and waxy-leafed creepers (think of the scenery in *Tarzan, Jurassic Park* and *The Jungle Book*). Many flowering vines from the subtropical world — like the Bougainvillea, Stephanotis, Antigonon and the Passiflora family — also do well in most tropical environments. Others, like the Scindapsus (the common Money Plant draped over filing cabinets around the world) and the Devil's Trumpet grow to heroic proportions in the Tropics and must be regularly trimmed off tree trunks and building walls if used. Manageable flowering vines, like the *Thunbergia grandiflora* (or *T. mysorensis*), help to guarantee full shade, when trained up Plumeria trees or pergolas, and also to create wonderful, long draping floral displays at the host tree's extremities.

Shade structures, like pergolas and trellises, are an important part of tropical garden design. Fast-growing vines help make timber latticework into an efficient and attractive sun block. Many hardy vines — the Allamanda, the *Bauhinia kockiana*, the Clerodendrum and Stephanotis — are wet-season flowerers and therefore prove very useful in planting schemes when everything else has turned green.

Creepers like *Monstera deliciosa*, the various climbing members of the colourful Philodendron family and the mighty *Ficus pumila* (or Dollar Vine) are most effective when used to soften a courtyard or "void" wall, as they tend to grow admirably in partial light. The flowering vines love lots of sunlight and are therefore useful in masking unsightly tennis court fences, and for trellis planting in general.

Like orchids and ferns, vines can be thought of as accessories, the addition of which, in the late planning stage, helps realize a fulsome, artful and natural look.

WATER PLANTS

ABOVE: Nymphaea capensis *water lilies in the water garden of the Villa Bebek.*

BELOW: Cressida Campbell's woodblock print of the main water garden at the Villa Bebek.

The architecture of ancient Egypt and India incorporated forms inspired by certain water plants: Egyptian buildings used bound papyrus or lotus forms for their columns; all Indian gods are depicted on holy water lily bases, called *padma.* The Buddha chose the beautiful, pink-petalled lotus as the symbol of his new faith as it "rose from the mud to reach the light".

The myth and magic surrounding water plants are as amazing as their biodiversity. Water plants can be huge, like the giant elephant-ear water caladiums, or the *Victoria amazonica* (formerly *Victoria regia*) water lilies (whose leaf pad can measure over 2 metres (6 ½ feet) in diameter, or tiny like the *Nymphoides indica* which "dances" on the water like a sugar-plum fairy. Water plants are extremely easy to transplant and propagate — provided there is enough sun and water.

There are many water plants which thrive in containers too — like water hyacinths and Iris. Dwarf-blue water lilies are found in terracotta urns in the temples of Bali (see photo page 35). Even the jewel-like lotus will grow in a metre-deep container of water half filled with water. They are also easily propagated from seeds. There are also many night-blooming varieties of water lilies ... something that is quite unique to the water-plant world.

Water plants can help to soften a water feature. Bogside flora — like the bulrush, papyrus and Iris — are excellent for softening the water's edge. Note that from the introduction of just one pink lotus, a pond of white lotuses can be quickly turn pink. Furthermore, some fish may nibble away water plants (ask your supplier). These pages show how water plants can balance the composition of a water garden and surrounding planting scheme. (See also the Water Gardens section.)

ABOVE: Water Lettuce (Pistia stratiotes), *bulrushes and a potted* Wrightia religiosa *make this unique water garden of andesite pots.*

LEFT: The leaves and "zig-zag" stems of this water plant bring a dash of light whimsy to this water garden planting scheme.

Chapter 8

TROPICAL GARDEN ART

" *While the creation of an interesting garden requires design and horticultural skills, a stylist's eye is needed when adding the artistic touches.* "

rtwork accents are the jewellery, shoes and bags of the tropical garden world, and the finishing touches in the search for the perfect blend of the natural and the man-made. While the creation of an interesting garden requires design and horticultural skills, a stylist's eye is needed when adding the artistic touches. These finishing touches — a statue or an urn at the end of a garden path, a pavilion folly sited in the grand English manner in a picturesque landscape — are the cherries on the cake. They catch the eye and prove the pudding: they add gaiety and wit to a naturalist's art.

One should not design a garden from a desire to incorporate a set piece but rather choose the right "accent" once the base creation is complete. If pavilions and pergolas are part of the garden design, they too should be treated as artworks and framed suitably. Most of all, the artwork should match the setting and enhance the appreciation of the overall design: scattering sculptures do not a garden make. One of my favourite gardens, that of garden-designers Dennis Allard and Sheila Carrol at Ilford House, which is their home in the Australian bush, features lovingly littered Victorian metal hobby horses and rusty toy cars amongst the wild grasses and poppy fields. Another favourite is Fontainebleau, outside Paris, where massive urns and topiary cones create "turns" in the otherwise rigid gardens laid out in formal French style. In the tropical world, I love the quirkish palace gardens of the Javanese sultans with their rare blend of chinoiserie, Dutch herbaceous borders and Moorish fountains, and the temple gardens of Bali where the boundaries between garden, art and architecture are delightfully fused.

It seems that throughout history rulers have engaged in creating great garden art — the Sphinx of Giza and Stonehenge are but two giant examples — and from these regal predecessors, one suspects, garden art has grown. One should look to the great artistic gardens, of the past and present, for inspiration — the repetition of other designers' tricks, in a new setting, is part of the tradition-passing process.

The placement of the artwork or pavilion is 90% of the job — getting the style of the piece right is the final brush stroke. Too much jewellery or the wrong shoes can spoil a great outfit, likewise can a well laid out garden be spoiled by inappropriate decoration. This may sound precious but the placement of art in a garden is a precise art. In this chapter I will try to give enough examples of the effect of many kinds of artworks in different surroundings. I will also touch on how the style of the architecture must influence the style of the garden, right down to the choice of materials and textures in the garden art.

Follies and ruinscapes are my passion, so I will give some examples of tropical versions of both. As the tropical world has lots of water bodies and far too much

ABOVE: A ceramic Chinese shrine settled amongst the palms and ferns of a suburban garden in Singapore.

OPPOSITE: A Jepun pedestal fountain, from the Wijaya Classics Range of garden artifacts, amidst a loose collection of carved Balinese soapstone panels at the Villa Bebek.

PAGE 168: Spouts from 17th-century Javanese Hindu temples in a museum in Trowulan, East Java.

PAGE 169, LEFT TO RIGHT: A wall in the Majorelle tropical garden in Marakesh; Sumba artworks on a fern encrusted compang *in the Villa Bebek; a coral wall with Boma gargoyle in a Sanur temple; guardian statues at the Villa Bebek kitchen.*

PAGES 170–71: A trio of gamelan player statues in the gardens of the Bali Hyatt hotel.

ABOVE, LEFT: The main reception court of the 17th-century Susuhana Palace in Surakarta, Central Java, boasts French statues that were presented by Queen Wilhelmina of the Netherlands 100 years ago.

OPPOSITE: A full-scale reproduction of the statue of Jayavarman VII (which is the centrepiece of the Phnom Penh National museum) in the garden of the author's Singapore house.

ABOVE, RIGHT: The art gallery-like garden of Surakarta-based gentleman aesthete, K.R.T. Hardjonegoro (Go Tik Swan).

RIGHT: A kul-kul drum tower folly at the entrance to the Bali Hyatt gardens in Sanur.

BELOW: Ornamental planters brimming with white cacti flank the spa entrance at the Four Seasons Resort, Bali.

sun, bridges and decorative shade structures will be featured in this artwork section too. Decorativism has been much maligned in the second half of the 20th century: the Art Deco, Post-Modern and Minimalist schools were all born out of a desire to get away from the root of decoration, in nature. As I write, from my Southeast Asian perch, confusion reigns on the subject of suitable artworks. Anything overtly decorative is today called "Balinese", despite the great minimalist traditions in Bali's mountain regions. "Too Oriental" is another catch-cry of the "New Asian". In most of the tropical world traditionalism is considered old-hat but, as Buckminster Fuller once wisely asked, "How do you know where you're going if you don't know where you've come from?" Brilliant Indian designer Rajiv Sety recently said, "Everyone's so busy going global, they've forgotten about local!"

My advice to the landscaper is don't be influenced by trends. Choose what you like and what you consider suitable. Gnome gardens look great in Switzerland, and topiary Bambis are not out of place in the heady kitchscapes of suburban Saigon.

Over the last 25 years in Bali I've watched road art progress from truly inspired, even Rodin-esque, stylized Hindu statues to 3-D cartoons of galloping white horses, the landscape equivalent to bimbo art on black velvet. The progression is an attempt by the proletariat to blaze forward, blindly, with the latest trends from overseas. Choose art and design artistic accents with a great respect for nature and for local artwork traditions: don't "gild the lily".

Glazed earthenware, carved stone and hardwood pots and urns decorate terraces and gardens throughout the Tropics – particularly Southeast Asia, where pedestal pots have been part of a decorative tradition for at least 1,000 years. The shapes can be traced back to the arrival of the first Hindu pilgrim priests from South India where pots of dwarf lotuses were kept in Brahman homes, to propagate lotus flowers for offerings; and the arrival of the first emissaries from Annam (Vietnam) where the glazed pot on a colourful shapely stand is a national institution, found in front of every government building to this day.

NEAR LEFT: Terracotta pots flank the entrance to the tomb of one of the holy Muslim saints of Java.

BELOW: A Nyuun Jun holy water vessel and pedestal, reinvented, in Bali, as a terrace artwork.

The propagation of potted plants and the "matching" of pot shape, to plant, and to the setting is one of the oldest art forms in history. The classic Vietnamese stand and bonsai pot (drawing below) inspired many copyists across the equator during the 16th–19th centuries, the renaissance era of landscape design in Southeast Asia. Most of the pots and stands shown left were designed by my office for various projects in Bali, Jakarta and Singapore, using local materials and design motifs. The photo bottom right is of a house in Galle, Sri Lanka.

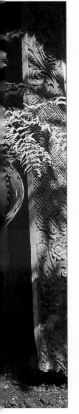

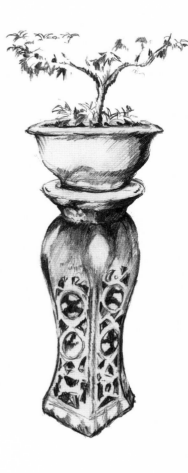

STATUES

A pair of singa *(lion)*
statues guard the
entrance court in
K.R.T. Hardjonegoro's
Surakarta home,
Central Java.

Having got this far into the book, and now on to my favourite gardening topic, that of decorative accents, I think I should be allowed to become a little bit autobiographical, if not confessional. And so I shall.

I love pixies.

Statues in gardens are, for me, nymphs and spirits. The placement of an anthropomorphic or even a totemic form is like raising a maypole at a country fair — the whole place comes to life. Statues are guardians of spirit and place and they keep us nature-lovers company during the long months of dealing with architects' reveals and thin grey stripes. A beautifully-formed and well-placed statue screams "Hallelujah!", "Ain't I gorgeous?" and "Isn't life wonderful?" Even those kitschy garden gnomes and the miniature pagodas placed in fish tanks bring a theatre of stories and romantic architectural models to the outside world. All of the images reproduced on this page are of guardian statues, seen in rather austere tropical settings, but this book is full of whimsical corners (see photograph page 2) and examples of pixies peering from the bushes. The Dutch-Australian painter Ian Van Wieringin taught me the charm of having groupings of statues or rocks "talking to each other," as it were, and he showed me the effect such gentle groupings have on a garden setting.

Carved panels often read as just decorative finishes, or accents, in the architecture; but standing forms, be they obelisks, votive statues, or just friendly frogs, have a dynamic presence — they invite us to participate. Standing statues also come in the form of totems, pedestals, dolmens, stelae, lingas, guardians and, in the grand durbar squares of Nepal, as towering *tugeh* (called *tugu* in Indonesia), the cosmic nail that connects the earth to the celestial sphere.

In tropical garden design, a porous stone statue can become a "nest" of ferns and orchids in the wet season — mossy patinas and creeping vines add allure to a striking form. Statues can, when thoughtfully placed, divide a court's "floor plan" into different areas and also "fill in" a composition, as viewed from an important window or doorway. Walled courts give a designer lots of opportunity for placing statues — on plinths in front of the wall, on the wall's pillars or gathered, in a group, under a courtyard tree. Flanking statues can define important entrances or changes of level. The French have even erected pairs of statues that commemorate a kiss! Statues that portray important religious icons should be used reverentially, or not at all: the tropical world is awash with "scatter Buddhas".

Today many cultures in tropical regions are wary of the use of figurative forms: to me this trend signifies the decline of a culture until only the superstitions remain. Celebrate life — place a statue today.

ABOVE: Batik impresario K.R.T. Hardjonegoro's traditional Javanese courtyard house in Surakarta, Central Java, is home to some magnificent statues displayed with elegant simplicity.

LEFT: Artist Putu Suarsa created this statue garden at the entrance to his Big Bamboo complex in South Bali.

Most Oriental gardens are thus named because of the artwork found within. The East is so rich in dynamic decorative traditions that it takes years of observation before all the curlicues and arabesques swim into focus. Haiti is a tropical island on the other side of the world with a rich decorative tradition too (see iron fretwork panel BELOW).

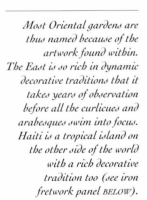

CLOCKWISE FROM BOTTOM RIGHT: *A carved soapstone panel in the Lanna Thai style of Northern Thailand set into a garden wall of pitted soapstone; a classical South Chinese air vent, carved out of granite, set in the wall of an Ernesto Bedmar designed house in Singapore; a polychromatic carved teak air vent panel, set in a plastered wall at the Warung Mie restaurant garden, Four Seasons Resort, Jimbaran, Bali; an early 20th-century Balinese temple statue and a rustic soapstone water urn in a small walled court in the Villa Bebek, Sanur; Haitian ironwork; a grouping of Timorese ancestor figures on a compang-like platform in the Villa Bebek; a large carved andesite tableau in the grounds of the Candi Sukuh (16th century), Central Java; a statue from Java's classic Hindu period set in a garden wall in a Jakarta house.*

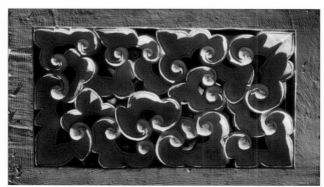

FOLLIES, GATES, PAVILIONS AND BRIDGES

Top: A simple Balinese gate with decorative accents by sculptor Wayan Cemul of Ubud, Bali, built as a romantic folly in a large garden I designed near Canggu in South Bali.

Above: A longhouse on a lake-like pond in Minangkabau, West Sumatra displays traditional glamour.

Right: Tony Duquette, designer of The King and I, *creates incredible follies in his Oriental gardens in the United States.*

Great gardens are made greater by the addition of a folly — that is, an exotic kiosk, pagoda, triumphal gate or a bridge that catches the eye. Medium and small gardens, can be considerably enhanced by the addition of a decorative gate or a tower whose function is primarily ornamental, but which may have other more practical uses. The *kul-kul* tower at the Villa Bebek, for example (see page 114), was conceived as a "vertical relief" folly, to balance the "flat" courtyard sprawl, and now houses a pump room and a water tank. Pavilion follies can also be belvederes and powder rooms (see photo page 188).

The most magnificent feature of the great works of landscape art in the Tropics over the past 500 years — Angkor Thom in Cambodia; the Summer Palace in Hue; the palace gardens of Mysore in South India — are the ornamental gates, providing dramatic backdrops for avenues of palms or shade trees. In the 20th century, "split gates" of Java and Bali temples have been copied, sometimes in mega proportions, and used in the entrance courts of grand hotels and resorts. Australian artist Donald Friend had an antique 18th-century *candi bentar* temple gate in his Sanur garden, as a folly, draped with an ancient bougainvillea vine. It was sublimely romantic, tucked away in his ravishing garden, with the Indian Ocean glimpsed through in the thick coastal planting.

The formula of the pavilion on the lake is another recurrent folly theme in South Indian, Southeast Asian and tropical colonial parkland design. The concept has lately been adapted in creating the "floating pavilions" (see pages 102–103) in many contemporary hotel and dream-house designs.

The rajas of old were great builders of follies — one thinks here of Tirta Gangga, in East Bali, with its ziggurat fountain (see photograph page 95); of the folly-like floating pagodas of Candi Kuning on Lake Bedugul high in the mountains of Bali; and of the magnificent white bathing pavilion built by the King of Ceylon in the 17th century on Kandy lake (which is itself man-made). Long parkland vistas in which to place a quirky "conversation piece" were more readily available, it would seem, in the days of yore.

Ruinscapes are a great form of folly too (see photo page 26). The required effect is easily and quickly achievable in the fecund Tropics where gardens can turn into romantic ruins after just one wet season.

Although not for every garden or budget, folly-building is one of the real treats of landscape design. If yearned for, it can be practised in micro scale, even in fish tanks, if it cannot be implemented on a macro scale. Miniature follies, faux gates and ruinscapes are all part of the theatrical magic, achievable on most budgets, that make a truly romantic tropical garden.

ABOVE, LEFT: The entrance walkway to the main dining room at the Four Seasons Resort, Bali, serves as a bridge over attractive water gardens.

ABOVE, RIGHT: A flaming gate designed by our office for a compound of rental villas called Puri Canggu Mertha, in Canggu, Bali.

LEFT: These three Asmat shields, framed by a Plumeria branch, create a dramatic artwork out of a simple wall at the Villa Bebek.

ABOVE: A Balinese garden gate designed by Pak Cekog of Taman, Sanur, for an estate at Batujimbar, Bali.

LEFT: A simple suspension bridge in a naturalistic garden becomes an artwork in this garden in the Philippines.

OPPOSITE: A "Majapahit" powder room in a lotus pond in a garden I designed in Singapore.

COMPANG

Compang is the Flores island's name for the raised platforms of stone, often pearl or oval-shaped, found in the main squares of the ancient Neolithic villages of Eastern Indonesia. They are most commonly used for meetings and ritual dances. In the older mountain villages of Bali, one also finds such platforms in the terraced sanctuaries that have now become Hindu temples. My old chum and garden mentor John Darling built a *compang* in his garden in the early 1980s and I was inspired to do a series, over the next 15 years, of "primitive" gardens with a *compang* as the central artwork. In my office courtyard garden in Bali, I have a small weedy *compang* under a very large *Pisonia alba*. It is "guarded" by some spirit effigies — sacred spring guardians, reputedly from Sumbawa, although I fear that they may well have been made in Kuta yesterday. The *compang* is surrounded by a collection of primitive art from the Asmat, the Tiwi of Northwestern Australia, Sumba in Eastern Indonesia and a modern landscape painting by Australian Jonathan Collard. *Compang* gardens look best with some modern art nearby: the sort of primitive-modern mix, which fuelled artists such as Picasso, le Corbusier and Brancuzzi, is particularly effective when used in tropical gardens.

RIGHT: I bought a gaggle of anthropomorphic "guardian" statues, ostensibly from a natural spring in Sumbawa, to "people" the compang *in the central modern-primitive court of the Villa Bebek. In 1998, I recreated the look, this time in limestone (LEFT) and added some coral to hide the pump valves in an internal garden court in the spa at the Four Seasons Resort, Bali.*

GARDEN FURNITURE

RIGHT: Good garden furniture should be able to stand alone as a work of art — likewise the positioning of the pieces should influence the overall garden design in an artful manner. This pair of cast-iron Art-Nouveau park benches, in a grove of Date Palms near the palace in Cordoba, Spain, are the only "artwork accent" in a sublimely simple garden.

In tropical houses, we tend to use garden spaces as outdoor "rooms" — design issues like space allocation and choice of garden furniture are therefore very important. The great Sri Lankan architect, Geoffrey Bawa, decorates the garden courts of his houses with modernist metal furniture that acts as both artwork accent and space definer. Bali-based designer Amir Rabik, whose alfresco parties are amongst the most star studded in the tropical world, invented a giant carved soapstone buffet table for his *soirées de gala* that also "shines" in the daytime like an important, if mossy, rococo commode. In the Villa Bebek, I always serve dinner in the garden under the broad-leaf canopy of a *Pisonia alba* tree, itself bedecked with moon orchids and epiphytes. Nearby, East Indonesian boundary markers, mushroom-like marvels of the Neolithic age, act as permanent occasional tables, whilst the dining table and chairs are moved out from the main house verandah. For special occasions, woven chandeliers are hung from tree branches and a quartet of string musicians (the popular *keroncong*) parked on a nearby garden bench. Guests enjoy vistas into the interiors from the garden. I even thought of building ha-has into the adjacent studio's floor so that dinner guests would not have their view spoiled by passing canines. Ha Ha!

But seriously, night entertaining in the garden is one of the joys of the tropical lifestyle so one should try to "capture the spirit" when designing a garden. I prefer a mix of permanent and "introduced" furniture (that is furniture carried out from inside) when entertaining in the garden. Everyday garden "set-ups" are a little sad if dominated by giant silent barbecues or groupings of empty plastic chairs. One has to achieve a balance between the aesthetic and the practical (see

page 192, Garden Lighting, and page 122, Pool Furniture, for further hints on this subject). Larger gardens may be enhanced by a wooden bench, and bungalow gardens a paved and furnished area away from the house to extend the space for entertaining.

More and more, people are putting large pieces of quasi-colonial "primitive" furniture in pebbled or paved tropical courts. These large decorative pieces make a big splash and are very useful as platforms for lounging or for siestas, as flower tables or for "sunning" herbs and spices. Personally, I love modern tropical courts which use slabs of stone or uncomplicated benches, wrapped around the railings, which can all be used for the same garden activities.

Just as the placement of garden furniture should be seen to enhance the overall beauty of the garden so the choice of plants and lighting needs to be carefully considered when designing an entertainment corner. For such areas, choose plants that keep their flowers at night — the Heliconias, the ginger family and the Thunbergias (*Thunbergia grandiflora* and *Lucretia thunbergia* are my favourites) — and those which have a nocturnal scent, such as the night-blooming cestrum. There are night-blooming versions of most water plants too. When dining with friends, it is inspiring to be partially under a tree, with its branches and leaves lit from below, and partially under the stars. Avoid garden furniture positions near septic tanks and trees that attract ants, obviously. Pergolas can become private dining rooms in the garden, if designed and decorated properly — the equivalent of the summer house or orangery in a temperate climate garden.

Choose your tropical garden furniture for durability as well — the monsoon months and the high degree of sunlight in the drier months quickly ruin all but the sturdiest designs. Timber furniture should be frequently oiled, if not painted, if that is the desired look; or at least put on dry plinths, like bricks in the grass, or a paved surface to avoid rot. Porous stone furniture, such as limestone, ages faster and tends to look more "compatible" in romantic garden settings than, say, shiny granites. Likewise moss outcrops look out of place in most modern tropical gardens. The urban street furniture of cities such as Singapore can be very hard on the bottom. Be brave with your choice of garden furniture, experiment but always remember: the white plastic garden chair is the antithesis of poetic garden design.

ABOVE: Another alternative for garden furniture (viable only if you have helpers) is to place indoor furniture outside. Bali-based designer Linda Garland has created many "opera box" terraces in the English garden tradition of putting garden benches at points with exceptional vistas.

BELOW: Poolside at the Villa Bebek, with 1920s-style garden furniture. (Sketch by Peter Wright.)

TROPICAL GARDEN LIGHTING

Our office designed this indoor garden in a Singapore terrace house in collaboration with local architect Chan Soo Khian. We provided the idea for the panels on the wall; he provided the spot lighting. The finished product is a good example of teamwork between architecture, interior, landscape and lighting design.

In the tropical world most house gardens have outdoor "entertainment" areas — a terrace, a patio, a pool deck — which can be used after dark.

With the sun going down at 6 p.m. unchangingly in most tropical places, one should make the most of dining out or entertaining under the stars, which can be done, weather permitting, 365 days a year. The lighting of these outdoor sitting rooms is therefore vital to creating an ambience that is both practical and pleasant, like an indoor living room. One doesn't always need enough light to find the car keys, but it's nice to see what one is eating. Candlelit dinners, *alfresco*, are among the great treats of the tropical lifestyle.

Gardens can look completely different in the moonlight. Clever lighting creates a mood as well as edits the big picture. Highlighting the strong forms and ideas — artworks, pavilions, courtyard walls — and leaving the unwanted in the dark, allows one to paint with light. Bodies of water can be left dark, for example, and allowed to reflect well-lit background plants or buildings. Lighting canopy trees from below creates a tent-like canopy of reflected light that is most attractive. The Japanese have shown us that a lantern light can be a thing of great beauty — it transfixes us with its ethereal glow. The Japanese are the masters of subtle lighting effects, as they rarely use too much.

How then to light one's own garden without getting a "Christmas tree" look?

There are two schools of aesthetic thought on tropical garden lighting: the Artificial Moonbeam School (A.M.S.) and the Soft Romantic Cosy (S.R.C.) schools. The former of these, the A.M.S., is popular in Hawaii, Singapore and Miami, where it can be afforded, and where people like it a bit bold and brassy. The S.R.C. School, however, is closer to the heart of the naturalists, of course, and allows real moonbeams a strong supporting role.

Personally I think there is a cut-off point, on luminaire-loading: if moonbeams on a full-moon night cease to cast shadows, then there's too much artificial light. That established, one can move onto the second tenet of good garden lighting: variety makes the heart grow fonder. Use a mixture of lanterns, pin-spots, floods and flares to achieve a well balanced lighting effect.

On an outdoor dining terrace, for example, you can provide an "ambient glow" on the perimeter, then pin-spot the odd artwork or nestle a spot under a big tree for that gorgeous uplighting effect. But always use candles on the table rather than the "railway marshalling-yard" effect of nasty floodlights. Glare is the enemy: one unshielded spot makes the pupil contract like a prodded sea anemone and all the other effects of gorgeous glow-lighting virtually disappear. *Balance* is the key-word, as it is in good interior lighting.

The landscape equivalent of a grid of halogen down spots playing in one's "awnings" is really rather grim.

In tropical houses or spaces where there is a lot of transparency — that is a lot of flow between interior and exterior spaces — it is extremely important to balance the lighting between the indoor and the outdoor spaces (the colonnades, verandahs and open pavilions). Courtyard spaces and the garden paths that link them are often part of an "interior" that just happens to be outside! Too many glamorous tropical houses and hotels suffer from either the wrong sort or of an imbalance of landscape lighting. If you like to live outside, learn how to balance the lighting design to satisfy your aesthetic and lifestyle requirements.

Three Steps to Better Tropical Garden Lighting

1. EVALUATE your garden environment. Is there a particularly handsome tree trunk to take a major up-light? Where would you be most likely to gather for a drink or a meal? You should plan to put a lantern-type lamp there. Which changes of level or steps need lighting? Is there a body of water or an artwork that can be utilized and lit for a dramatic night-time effect?

2. EXPERIMENT. Get a few waterproof garden spotlights. (Use a 12-volt system if children are likely to be around often when the power is on.) Attach long cables and try shooting them up trees and into pavilion voids, or down verandah columns and stairs to gauge the effect. You should have a basic lighting design in your head by this stage — experimenting helps to fine tune for minimum glare and maximum effect. Try putting spotlights in urns or garden pots to shield the flood light upwards. Likewise bollard or ground glow lights can be put behind a rock or at the base of a thick leafy shrub. Remember: yellow- and white-leafed plants take light best. Palms also look elegant if lit from below.

3. ELABORATE. Try using your garden or courtyard in different ways — for meals, for after-dinner coffee, for quiet chats — and test that the lighting is adequate for these different uses and that there is no glare felt from these "activity areas". Fine tune the nocturnal ambience by adding "shields" to hide the glare, or by adding fine pin spots to accent artworks, which will in turn glow with dazzling luminescent effect. If there is a body of water and a spout or fountain, an in-water light will throw "dancing shadows" upwards which adds "life". However, beware: if the pool is "static", underwater lights can serve to unnecessarily highlight the murkiness of the water, so experiment first.

Avoid nailing lights to trees or putting them anywhere that the power cable might be visible (as in trailing up a tree trunk or boundary wall).

TOP: In 1996 we worked on a small house in Singapore with architect Chan Soo Khian. The garden lighting was well integrated into the end pavilion's interior lighting which leached out into the swimming pool area.

ABOVE: Hanging and standing lanterns in our Singapore office garden. Again the potentially beneficial effect of light leaching out from the interiors can be seen.

a

e

f

b

c

∂

In 1996, architect Ken Vais worked with our office on the design of some garden lights that were "historically referenced" but contemporary in flavour. These designs and others become known as the Wijaya Classics Range. FROM TOP LEFT: (a) A Moorish-modern fibreglass dome glows in a nest of leafy foliage; (b) a bronze lantern inspired by social-realist chevron shapes on a museum wall in South China; (c) a heavy iron brazier designed by Bill Bensley; (∂) a pair of "spot-ups" in a simple terracotta pot; (e) our best seller, the hanging Sarang Burung lamp made of hand-beaten bronze; (f) an architectonic, version of the hanging lantern concept; (g) our standing Aeng lantern made of hand-beaten bronze with a fibreglass inner shell and a colourful glazed ceramic hat — it was inspired by a Japanese cut-paper design; (h) a pair of gas tiki lamps in an Hawaiian garden; (i) the caping lantern at our Singapore office;

PAGES 196–197: Cannons and topiary — an unlikely decorative mix, found here on the streets of Saigon.

g

h

i

APPENDIX 2

TREES AND SHRUBS THAT FLOWER IN THE WET SEASON

When planning the planting scheme in a tropical garden be sure to add a few "wet-season flowers" so that your garden isn't all green throughout the year. Think of the shapes of the shrubs, their leaves and their wet-season growing patterns too, as in the wet months a tropical garden relies on shapes and silhouettes for dramatic effect. Leaf colour and flowers tend to disappear with the diminishing of full sunlight.

The following is a list of my favourite wet-season flowers

Spathodea or African Tulip Tree
This stately specimen, easy to transplant, is a magnificent pomegranate red, ruffled, corsage-like bloom for most of the wet season.

Caesalpinia or Peacock Bush
This small tree–like shrub with its fine leaves grows to 2–3 metres (6 1/2–10 feet) overall height and presents magnificently throughout the wet months. There are red, pink, white varieties and a soft peach colour, known as Barbados Delight.

Allamanda
A hardy climber with waxy dark green leaves that literally "takes off" in the wet season, smothering Plumerias and pergolas with large clusters of trumpet-shaped daffodil-yellow flowers. It needs to be chopped back at the end of the wet season.

Thunbergia grandiflora
This rampant vine, my favourite pergola vine, continues to flower, like the lowly *Hibiscus rosa sinensis,* for the first two months of the wet season, and then should be cut back to encourage better "spring" flowering.

Mussaenda alba
The white-flowered variety of this popular shrub, which can grow to 4 metres (13 feet) in height, flowers only in the wet season, unlike its pink and red cousins. Used near white pampas grass and the other wet season presenters, like *Plumeria obtusa* and white oleander, one can create a scene that is crisp and almost "wintery" — that is, shrubs tinged with white.

Tiger lilies
In tropical countries the tiger lily family is dormant until the rains come and then they pop out, screaming for attention.

Rhoeo
The pretty white flower of the *Rhoeo* plant, the tropical gardeners bread and butter ground cover, appears at the base of the leaf clusters only at the beginning of the rainy months.

Hemigraphis
The plum-coloured Hemigraphis likewise has a pretty snowflake-like flower in the wet months.

Water lilies
Many water lilies seem to adore the wet season — one should add some of these (ask your supplier) to a pond planting scheme to ensure some colour and prettiness.

Vines
The *Gloriosa superba* beach vine, with its springy, orchid-like, canary yellow flower (and flaming red tips) is my favourite wet season flower.

OTHERS:
Cassia spectabilis
Kassumba (*Bixa orellana***)**
Alpinia (*Alpinia pupurata***)**
Shrimp Plants (*Pachystachys lutea***)**
Caraka (*Saraca indica***)**
Jatropha pandiflora
Heliconias
Plumeria obtusa
Moon Orchids (*RIGHT***)**

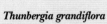

Bromeliads   Costus speciosa   *Wringthia*

Fiery Red Ginger   *Torch Ginger*   *Spider Lily*

BIBLIOGRAPHY

- **Akihary, drs. H,** 1996, *Ir. F.J.L. Ghijsels – Architect in Indonesia (1910–1929)*, Seram Press. Utrecht
- **Baldon, Cleo Melchior, Ib,** 1997, *Reflection on The Pool*, Rizzoli International Publications Inc. New York
- **Beamish, Jane Ferguson,** 1989, *A History of Singapore Architecture*, Graham Brash P/l. Singapore
- **Benjamin, Roger,** 1997, *Orientalism,* The Art Gallery of New South Wales. Sydney
- **Berry, Fred and Kress, W. John,** 1991, *Heliconia — An Identification Guide,* Smithsonian Institution Press. London
- **Binney, Marcus,** 1987, *Casas Nobres De Portugal,* M.T. Train-Scala Books, Nova Iorque. Lisbon
- **Boisselier, Jean,** 1989, *Majapahit,* Beurdeley and Cie. Paris
- **Bruggeman, L,** 1948, *Indisch Tuinboek,* Uitgevers Bedrijf 'De Spieghel'. Amsterdam.
- **Byfield, Graham and Liu, Gretchen,** 1995, *Singapore Sketchbook – The Restoration of a City,* Archipelago Press. Singapore
- **Carpenter, Bruce,** 1997, *W.O.J. Nieuwenkamp – First European Artist in Bali,* Archipelago Press. Singapore
- **Carpenter, Bruce,** 1993, *Willem Hofker – Painter of Bali,* Pictures Publishers. Wijk en Aalburg
- **Chin Kon Yit and Chen Voon Fee,** 1998, *Kuala Lumpur – A Sketchbook,* Archipelago Press. Singapore
- **Eliovson, Sima,** 1991, *The Gardens of Robert Burle Marx,* Saga Press Inc. Singapore
- **Fontein, Jan,** 1990, *The Sculpture of Indonesia,* Board of Trustees, National Gallery of Art. Washington
- **Griffiths, Tom,** 1994, *The Swimming Pool,* Michael Friedman Publishing Group Inc. New York
- **Hanna, Dr. Willard A.,** 1997, *Banda, A Journey Through Indonesia's Fabled Isles of Fire and Spice,* Yayasan Warisan dan Budaya Banda. Bali
- **Hanna, Dr. Willard A. and Alwi, Des,** 1990, *Turbulent Times Past in Ternate and Tidore,* Rumah Budaya Banda Naira Moluccas. East Indonesia
- **Haruzo, Ohashi,** 1987, *The Indoor Garden,* Graphic-Sha Publishing Co. Ltd. Tokyo
- **Helmi, Rio and Walker, Barbara,** 1995, *Bali Style,* Times Editions Pty. Ltd. Singapore
- **Hibbard, Don and Franzen, David,** 1986, *The View From Diamond Head. Royal Residence to Urban Resort,* Editions Limited. Honolulu, Hawaii

- **Hobhouse, Penelope,** 1997, *Natural Planting,* Pavilion Books Limited. London
- **Hobhouse, Penelope,** 1997, *Plants in Garden History,* Pavilion Books Limited. London
- **Holttum, R.E. and Enoch, Ivan,** 1991, *Gardening in the Tropics,* Times Editions Pty. Ltd. Singapore
- **Humphries, Barry,** 1980, *Treasury of Australian Kitsch,* Macmillan Pty Ltd. Melbourne
- **Jekyll, Gertrude and Weaver, Lawrence,** 1981, *Arts and Crafts Gardens,* Garden Art Press. London
- **Jessup, Helen I.,** 1997, *Angkor. Et Dix Siecles d'Art Khmer,* Editions de la Reunion des Musees Nationaux. Paris
- **Jessup, Helen I.,** 1990, *Court Arts of Indonesia,* The Asia Society Galleries. New York
- **Kaye, Myriam,** 1990, *An Illustrated Guide to Bombay and Goa,* The Guidebook Company Limited. Hong Kong
- **Kempers, A.J. Bernet,** 1959, *Ancient Indonesian Art,* C.P.J Van Der Peet. Amsterdam
- **Ledward, Daphne** (introduction only), 1995, *The Victorian Garden Catalogue. A Treasure Trove of Horticultural Paraphernalia,* Studio Editions Ltd. London
- **Lim Jee Yuan,** 1987, *The Malay House,* Institut Masyarakat Malaysia. Pulau Pinang
- **Macmillan, H.F.,** 1991, *Tropical Planting and Gardening,* Malayan Nature Society. Kuala Lumpur
- **Mari, Bartomeu,** 1993, *Les Jardins de Jacques Wirtz,* Fondation pour L'Architecture. Brussels
- **Michoutouchkine, N.,** 1989, *Ethnography and Art of Oceania,* Sojuzreclam Cultura U.S.S.R. Moscow
- **Moojen, P.A.J.,** 1926, *Bali,* Adi Poestaka. The Hague
- **Moore, Charles W.; Mitchel, William J. and Turnbull, William J.R.,** 1988, *The Poetics of Gardens,* The M.I.T. Press. London
- **Moreno, Francisco Prieto,** 1983, *Los Jardines De Granada,* Arte De Espana. Madrid
- **Perez, Rodrigo; Encarnacion, Rosario and Dacanay, Julian,** 1989, *Folk Architecture,* GCF Books. Manila
- **Pinto, Alberto,** 1992, *Alberto Pinto,* Michel Aveline Editeur. Paris
- **Plumptre, George,** 1993, *The Water Garden,* Thames and Hudson Ltd. London
- **Powell, Robert,** 1996, *The Tropical Asian House,* Select Books Pty. Ltd. Singapore

- **Pucci, Idanna,** 1985, *The Epic of Life,* Alfred Van Der Mark, Inc. New York
- **Raulet, Sylvie,** 1996, *Maharajas' Palaces,* Editions Hazan. Paris
- **Rhodius, Hans and Darling, John,** 1980, *Walter Spies and Balinese Art,* Terra, Zutphen/Tropical Museum. Amsterdam
- **Slesin, Suzanne and Cliff, Stafford,** 1985, *Caribbean Style,* Thames and Hudson Ltd. London
- **Smithers, Peter,** 1995, *Adventures of A Gardener,* The Harvill Press. London
- **Soebadio, Dr. Haryati,** 1996, ed., *Ancient History,* Indonesian Heritage Series, Buku Antar Bangsa. Jakarta.
- **Soebadio, Dr. Haryati,** 1996, ed., *Plants,* Indonesian Heritage Series, Archipelago Press. Singapore
- **Sosrowardoyo, Tara; Schoppert, Peter and Damais, Soedarmadji,** 1997, *Java Style,* Archipelago Press. Singapore
- **Streatfield, David C.,** 1994, *California Gardens – Creating a New Eden,* Abbeville Press. Singapore
- **Street-Porter, Tim,** 1981, *Interiors,* Omnibus Press. London
- **Street-Porter, Tim,** 1989, *Casa Mexicana. The Architecture, Design and Style of Mexico,* Stewart, Tabori, and Chang, Inc. New York
- **Taylor, Brian Brace,** 1986, *Geoffrey Bawa,* Concept Media Pty. Ltd. Singapore
- **Taylor, Jennifer,** 1986, *Australian Architecture Since 1960,* The Law Book Company Limited. Sydney
- **Tettoni, Luca Invernizzi,** 1998, *Myanmar Style. Art, Architecture and Design of Burma,* Periplus Editions (HK) Ltd. Hong Kong
- **Tettoni, Luca Invernizzi and Warren, William,** 1996, *Thai Garden Style,* Periplus Editions (HK). Hong Kong
- **Tettoni, Luca Invernizzi, and Warren, William,** 1995, *Balinese Gardens,* Periplus Editions (HK) Ltd. Hong Kong
- **Uhl, Natalie W. and John Dransfield,** 1987, *Genera Palmarum,* Allen Press Inc. Lawrence, Kansas
- **Wachlin, Steven,** 1994, *Woodbury and Page,* KTLV Press. Leiden
- **Warren, William,** 1991, *The Tropical Garden,* Thames and Hudson Ltd. London
- **Waterson, Roxana,** 1990, *The Living House. An Anthropology of Architecture in South-East Asia,* Oxford University Press Pty. Ltd. Kuala Lumpur

GAZETTEER

MAJOR DESIGN WORK BY MADE WIJAYA AND P.T. WIJAYA TRIBWANA INTERNATIONAL 1978–99

YEAR	PROJECT	PAGE (PHOTO OR ILLUSTRATION)	LANDSCAPE CONTRACTOR
1978	House "C" Batujimbar, Bali	105, 140, 189	C.V. Swastika Kebun
	Wantilan Lama Batujimbar Estates, Sanur, Bali	19, 124	C.V. Swastika Kebun
	Muller House, Ubud, Bali		C.V. Swastika Kebun
1979	La Taverna Hotel, Sanur, Bali		C.V. Swastika Kebun
	Jero Kubu, Sanur (landscape and architecture)	20	C.V. Swastika Kebun
	Narmada Hotel, Sanur, Bali		C.V. Swastika Kebun
1980	Bali Hyatt, Sanur, Bali	Back Cover, 10, 18, 19, 43, 50, 60, 63, 69, 71, 90, 98, 136, 137, 141, 144, 145, 146, 150, 155, 157, 161, 170, 173	C.V. Swastika Kebun
	Bali Sanur Bungalows (4 hotels), Sanur, Bali		C.V. Swastika Kebun
1981	The Oberoi, Bali	79	C.V. Swastika Kebun & P.T. Indosekar
	Hyatt Aryaduta, Jakarta		P.T. Indosekar
	U.S. Ambassador's Residence, Jakarta		P.T. Indosekar
	Salman-Frost House, Jakarta		C.V. Swastika Kebun
	Batujimbar Estates (15 villas), Sanur, Bali		C.V. Swatika Kebun & P.T. Indosekar
	Hertz House, Sayan, Bali (landscape and architecture)		C.V. Swatika Kebun & P.T. Indosekar
1982	Hotel Bualu, Nusa Dua, Bali		C.V. Swastika Kebun
	Agnes Montenay Cottage, Sayan, Bali (landscape and architecture)	12, 52	P.T. Indosekar
	White Garden and Gading Garden, Bali Hyatt	146, 150	P.T. Indosekar
	Australian Consulate, Bali		P.T. Indosekar
	Tjiptobiantoro House, Jakarta (upgrade)		P.T. Indosekar
1983	Hyatt Regency, Surabaya	20, 49	P.T. Indosekar
	Jakarta Hilton		P.T. Indosekar
	Brawa Development (6 houses), Brawa, Bali (landscape and architecture)	184	P.T. Indosekar
	Menaro House, Surabaya, Java		P.T. Indosekar
	Selby House, Jakarta		P.T. Indosekar
1985	Saba Bay Resort, Bali (landscape, architecture and interiors)	17	P.T. Indosekar
	La Taverna, Sanur, Bali		P.T. Indosekar
	Hotel Bualu, Nusa Dua, Bali		P.T. Indosekar
	Edleson House, Jakarta		P.T. Indosekar

YEAR	PROJECT	PAGE (PHOTO OR ILLUSTRATION)	LANDSCAPE CONTRACTOR
	Pangkey House, Surabaya, Java		P.T. Indosekar
	Harmoko House, Jakarta	72	P.T. Indosekar
1986	Amandari Hotel, Ubud, Bali	43, 58, 106, 108	P.T. Indosekar
	David Salman House, Jakarta		P.T. Indosekar
	U.S. Ambassador's Residence, Jakarta		P.T. Indosekar
	French Ambassador's Residence, Jakarta		P.T. Indosekar
1987	Hyatt Aryaduta, Jakarta		P.T. Indosekar
	David Bowie House, Mustique, West Indies	102, 118	P.T. Indosekar
	Villa Bebek, Sanur, Bali (landscape, architecture and interiors)	Cover, 6, 8, 21, 44, 48, 49, 50, 55, 57, 62, 64, 68, 69, 73, 74, 75, 76, 77, 99, 114, 123, 139, 144, 147, 156, 159, 166, 167, 169, 172, 182, 184, 187, 191, 194, 198	P.T. Indosekar
1988	Höfer House, Singapore	91, 158	P.T. Indosekar
	Australian Ambassador's Residence, Jakarta		P.T. Indosekar
1989	Taman Bebek Villas, Sayan, Ubud, Bali, (landscape, architecture, and interiors)	12, 53, 54, 79, 84, 85, 121, 159, 165	P.T. Indosekar
	Sampoerna House, Surabaya, Java		P.T. Indosekar
	Basil's Too Discoteque, St. Vincent, West Indies		P.T. Indosekar
1990	Hyatt Regency, Perth, Australia (upgrade)		P.T. Indosekar
	Mitsubishi House, Singapore		Pacific Nature Pte. Ltd.
	Sampoerna House, Surabaya		P.T. Indosekar
	New Australian Embassy, Jakarta		P.T. Indosekar
1991	Dai-Ichi Hotel, Jakarta		P.T. Indosekar
	Murdoch House, Sayan, Bali (landscape and architecture)		P.T. Indosekar
1992	Four Seasons Resort, Jimbaran, Bali	2, 35, 63, 84, 86, 92, 96, 104, 117, 118, 119, 120, 126, 134, 141, 164, 165, 185, 188	P.T. Indosekar
	Ng Ser Miang House, Singapore	195	Pacific Nature Pte. Ltd.
	Harmoko House, Jakarta	72	P.T. Indosekar
	341 Dahan Road, Singapore	175	Pacific Nature Pte. Ltd.
	Pek House, Singapore		Pacific Nature Pte. Ltd.
1993	B.P. House, Singapore		Pacific Nature Pte. Ltd.
	Australian Embassy, Jakarta		P.T. Indosekar
	Probosutedjo House, Jakarta	73	P.T. Indosekar
1994	Hyatt Regency, Singapore (Roof Garden)	78, 81, 88	Pacific Nature Pte. Ltd.
	Santika Beach Hotel, Bali		P.T. Indosekar

YEAR	PROJECT	PAGE (PHOTO OR ILLUSTRATION)	LANDSCAPE CONTRACTOR
	House XX, Singapore	39	Pacific Nature Pte. Ltd.
	Culture Centre, Sentul, Jakarta		P.T. Indosekar
	House XXVI, Singapore	192	Pacific Nature Pte. Ltd
	Bird House, Singapore		Pacific Nature Pte. Ltd
1995	Hsieh Fu Hua House, Singapore		Pacific Nature Pte. Ltd
	URA Roof Garden, Singapore	89	Pacific Nature Pte. Ltd
	House, Singapore XX	73, 80, 112, 174	Pacific Nature Pte. Ltd
	Nusa Dua Spa, Nusa Dua Bali		P.T. Indosekar
	Bali Intercontinental Hotel, Jimbaran, Bali (replanting)		P.T. Indosekar
	House XXX, Singapore	193	Pacific Nature Pte. Ltd
1996	Grand Bali Beach Hotel, Sanur, Bali	35, 115	P.T. Indosekar
	Nusa Dua Beach Hotel, Bali	115	P.T. Indosekar
	Goodwood Park Hotel, Singapore (Pool Court)		Pacific Nature Pte. Ltd.
	Alnjo House, Senopati, Jakarta	57, 126	P.T. Sekar Watu Damar
	Dr. C.C. Lau, Singapore		Pacific Nature Pte. Ltd
	Pacific Nature Office, Singapore	70	P.T. Indosekar
	Ganesha Gallery, Four Seasons Resort, Jimbaran Bay, Bali	105	P.T. Indosekar
	Aston Hotel, Tanjung, Nusa Dua		P.T. Indosekar
	Health Club and Spa, Four Seasons Resort Jimbaran Bay, Bali	127, 128, 129, 174, 186	P.T. Indosekar
	Garden Plaza Hotel, Saigon, Vietnam		Pacific Nature Pte. Ltd.
	New Von Bueren House, Brawa, Bali		P.T. Indosekar
1997	Canggu Puri Mertha Hotel, Canggu, Bali, (landscape, architecture and interiors)	57, 185	P.T. Indosekar
	Sheraton Bandara Hotel, Airport, Jakarta	189	P.T. Sekar Watu Damar
	Le Meridien Jakarta (Taman Sari Swimming Pool)	117	P.T. Sekar Watu Damar
	The Leela, Bombay, India (upgrade)		P.T. Wijaya
	Leela Beach Goa, India (upgrade)		P.T. Wijaya
	Victor Ngo House, Singapore	119, 188	Pacific Nature Pte. Ltd.
	Woollerton Appartments, Singapore	193	Pacific Nature Pte. Ltd.
	Wee Ee Lim House, Singapore		Pacific Nature Pte. Ltd.
	Dr. Cheong House, Singapore		Pacific Nature Pte. Ltd.
	Amy Lee House, Singapore		Pacific Nature Pte. Ltd.
	Abimanyu House, Jakarta		P.T. Sekar Watu Damar
	Pulau Seribu, Mr. David Salman (landscape and architecture)		P.T. Indosekar
	Kemang House, Jakarta		P.T. Sekar Watu Damar
	Milo House, Seminyak, Kuta		P.T. Indosekar
	Santika Menado, North Sulawesi		P.T. Sekar Watu Damar
	Soetikno Soedarjo House, Jakarta	118	P.T. Sekar Watu Damar
	Istana Tunku Abu Bakar, Johor, Malaysia		P.T. Sekar Watu Damar

YEAR	PROJECT	PAGE (PHOTO OR ILLUSTRATION)	LANDSCAPE CONTRACTOR
	Ganesha Gallery, Four Seasons Resort, Jimbaran, Bali	105	P.T. Indosekar
1998	Warung Mie, Four Seasons Resort, Jimbaran, Bali (landscape, architecture and interiors)	104, 182	P.T. Indosekar
	Regent of Jakarta (upgrade)		P.T. Sekar Watu Damar
	Robert Yeoh House, Kuala Lumpur, Malaysia		Pacific Nature Pte. Ltd.
	Azizan House Kuala Lumpur, Malaysia		Pacific Nature Pte. Ltd.
	Victor Ngo House, Kuala Lumpur, Malaysia		Pacific Nature Pte. Ltd.
	Srinivasan House, Chennai, India		Owner
	Lim Kian Onn House, Kuala Lumpur	39	Pacific Nature Pte. Ltd.
	South East Asian Studies Building, Singapore		Pacific Nature Pte. Ltd.
	Puri Canggu Mertha	57, 205	P.T. Indosekar
1999	Locklin House, Hualalai Resort, Hawaii		Robert Frost Landscaping
	Azizan House, Kuala Lumpur, Malaysia		Pacific Nature Pte. Ltd.
	Mahathir House, Kuala Lumpur, Malaysia		Pacific Nature Pte. Ltd.
	Kemang House, Jakarta		P.T. Sekar Watu Damar
	49 Black Sands Beach, Mauna Lani Resort, Hawaii		n/a
	Lassen House, Kapalua, Maui, Hawaii		n/a
	Ow House, Vaucluse, Sydney, Australia		n/a
	Tow Houses, Singapore		Pacific Nature Pte. Ltd.

ABOVE AND RIGHT: Puri Canggu Mertha, Bali (architecture, Interiors and landscape by P.T. Wijaya). Drawings by Stephen Little.

P.T. WIJAYA TRIBWANA INTERNATIONAL
Villa Bebek
Jl. Pengembak No. 9B Mertasari, Sanur 80228, Bali, Indonesia
Ph.: 62 361 287668, 287632   Fax: 62 361 286731
E-mail: ptwijaya@dps.mega.net.id or ptwijaya@indosat.net.id
Home page: http://www.wijaya.com

Addresses of Landscape Contractors :

■ PT. Sekar Watu Damar
Jl. Tebet Barat Dalam IV G No. 5
Jakarta Selatan 12810, Indonesia
Ph. : 62 21 835 7165, 830 3119
Fax. : 62 21 835 7166
E-mail : pteswede@centrin.net.id

■ P.T. Tribwana Indosekar
Jl. Mertasari No. 42, Suwung Kangin,
Denpasar 80224, Bali, Indonesia
Ph. : 62 361 720946
Fax. : 62 361 720507
E-mail : tribwana@dps.mega.net.id

■ Pacific Nature Landscape Pte. Ltd
Plot 2 No. 15 PSA Nursery
Joan Road, Singapore 298899
Ph. : 65. 252 2136
Fax. : 65 251 1970
E-mail : pacnat@pacific.net.sg

■ Queen Construction
and Robert Frost Landscaping
P.O. Box 1560 Honoaa, HI 96727
Ph. : 1 808 775 8043
Pager : 1 808 898 3283
Cell Ph. : 1 808 987 5452

IMPORTANT AND GREAT TROPICAL GARDENS MENTIONED IN THIS BOOK

AUSTRALIA
- Brisbane Botanic Gardens, Brisbane
- Cairns Botanic Gardens, Cairns, Queensland
- Townsville Botanic Gardens, Townsville, Queensland

CAMBODIA
- Phnom Penh Museum, Angkor Wat, Siem Reap (10 minutes from Siem Reap)

CHINA
- Kunming Botanic Garden, Kunming, Yunan (20 minutes from town centre)

INDIA
- The Madras Club, Chennai

INDONESIA
Java
- Taman Sari, Yogyakarta, Central Java (city centre)
- Taman Raya Bogor (Indonesian Botanic Garden), Bogor, West Java (1 hour East of Jakarta)
- Presidential Palace, Bogor, West Java
- Taman Raya Cibodas, Cibodas, West Java

Bali
- Bali Bird Park, Singapadu (45 minutes from airport)
- Bali Hyatt Horticultural Garden, Bali Hyatt Hotel, Sanur (30 minutes from airport)
- Linda Garland Estate (Bamboos), Nyuh Kuning, Ubud (private)
- Four Seasons Resort Bali, Jimbaran (10 minutes from Ngurah Rai airport)
- Tirta Gangga, Karangasem, East Bali (10 minutes from Amplapura)
- Taman Ujung, Ujung, East Bali (10 minutes from Amlapura
- Pura Batu Karo, Tabanan (30 minutes north of Tabanan, in the mountains)
- Eka Karya Botanic Gardens, Bedugul, Singaraja
- Tirta Empul, Tampaksiring
- Goa Gajah (Elephant Cave), Bedulu

Lombok
- Taman Mayura, Cakranegara (city centre)
- Taman Narmada, Narmada (10 minutes outside Cakranegara)

Spice Islands
- Banda Neira

MALAYSIA
- Penang Arboretum, Penang (one hour from Penang airport)
- Penang Botanic Garden, Penang (45 minutes from Penang airport)
- Taman Negara, Pahang, (1 hour from Kuala Lumpur airport)

MYANMAR
- Yangon Botanic Garden, Yangon

NETHERLANDS
- The Green House, Leiden Hortus Botanicus (the world's oldest) (town centre)

PHILIPPINES
- Zobel Alaya Estate, Catalagan (private)
- Manila Botanic Gardens, Manila (city centre)

SINGAPORE
- Singapore Botanic Gardens (city centre)
- Singapore Zoo (45 minutes from airport)
- Grand Hyatt Singapore (city centre)
- Shangri-la Hotel (city centre)
- Mandai Garden

SRI LANKA
- Sri Lanka Botanic Garden "Peradeniya", Kandy (15 minutes outside Kandy)

- Others:
All Geoffrey Bawa's hotels and the New Oriental Hotel in Galle

THAILAND
- Bangkok Botanic Garden, Bangkok
- Bangkok's National Museum, Bangkok
- Prasart Museum, The Ancient City
- Thai Buddhist Temple, Petchburi
- The Siwalai Garden, Bangkok's Grand Palace, Bangkok
- Vimarn Mek Palace, Bangkok

USA
Florida, Miami
- Fairchild Tropical Garden

Hawaii
- Allerton Garden, Kauai (also called the Pacific Botanic Gardens) (1 hour from airport)
- Four Seasons Resort Kaupulehu, Kapalua (110 minutes from Kona airport)
- Hilo Botanic Garden, Hilo, Hawaii (15 minutes from Hilo airport)
- Lyon's Arboretum (city centre)
- Foster Gardens, Honolulu (city centre)
- Queen Emma's Garden, Honolulu (on the Pilo Highway, city centre)
- Queen Lili'uokalani Garden (on the Pilo Highway)
- The Contemporary Museum Garden, Honolulu
- University of Hawaii campus
- May Moir House
- Leland Miyano Garden, Koolaus, Oahu

VIETNAM
- Ho Chi Minh City Botanic Garden, Ho Chi Minh City
- Hue Summer Palace, Hue (city centre)

WEST INDIES
- St Vincent Botanic Garden; Bridgetown, St Vincent (5 minutes from town)
- Pamplemousses Botanic Garden, Martinique

SUBTROPICAL GARDENS OF INTEREST (OR GARDENS WITH SUBTROPICAL SECTIONS)

AUSTRALIA
- Sydney Botanic Gardens (Palm section; Subtropical Glass House), Sydney
- Centennial Park, Paddington (Palm and Bamboo section), Chinese Garden, Darling Harbour, Sydney
- Kings Park, Perth, Western Australia

CHINA
- Quandong Botanic Gardens, Quandong, Quanchou

UK
- The Palm House, Kew, London
- Tresco Gardens, Isles of Scilly

USA
- Huntington Gardens, Pasadena, California

Other countries with tropical garden traditions of considerable importance: Brazil, Mexico, Venezuela, Jamaica, Panama, Colombia, Bolivia, South Africa, Mozambique, Seychelles, Reunion Islands, Mauritius (especially Pamplemousses Botanic Gardens).

INDEX